P9-DGG-658

PUBLIC OPINION AND THE SPANISH-AMERICAN WAR

A STUDY IN WAR PROPAGANDA

PUBLIC OPINION AND THE SPANISH-AMERICAN WAR

A STUDY IN WAR PROPAGANDA

BY

MARCUS M. WILKERSON, PH.D.
Associate Professor of Journalism,
Louisiana State University

NEW YORK / RUSSELL & RUSSELL

FIRST PUBLISHED 1932
REISSUED, 1967 BY RUSSELL & RUSSELL
A DIVISION OF ATHENEUM HOUSE, INC.
L.C. CATALOG CARD NO.: 66-24770

PRINTED IN THE UNITED STATES OF AMERICA

64777

To Helen

CONTENTS

INTRODUCTION

War propaganda is perhaps as old as war itself, though in recent years means for its dissemination have been perfected with the same genius that has improved and made more deadly the implements of war. In ancient times war propaganda was spread by word of mouth; today all the resources of a highly mechanized civilization are mobilized to sway the public mind.

War propaganda is an insidious thing. Once started it gains momentum with success until truth and rational thought are left stranded upon the reefs of discord and strife. Like the sleeping sickness of the tropics, its influence steals upon us until we become enmeshed in the coils of prejudice and hatred and join in the preachment of exaggerations and half truths. Lies become a part of the munitions of war.

In this study an attempt has been made to show the influence of the American press in causing opposition to Spanish rule in Cuba and finally in bringing about the intervention of the United States in the island. The rapid succession of Cuban revolts against Spanish rule, of which there were eight in the period between 1823 and 1855, followed by a prolonged conflict known as the "Ten Years' War," 1868-1878, and the "Little War" in 1883, led to the belief in the United States that the rapidly declining monarchy of Spain would never be able to control the island. Each outbreak was put down with severity, but with each succeeding uprising sympathy for the rebels increased. The revolutions were regarded as contests for independence, and the proximity of the island to this country accentuated the benevolent attitude of Americans. Despite this feeling, however, it is doubtful if many Americans favored the use of force to effect Cuba's freedom.

The story of how the people of the United States, embroiled with political and economic issues following the severe financial depression of 1893, were led to war with a third rate European power in behalf of a group of Cubans, many of whom were illiterate and about whom little was known except what had been published in newspaper reports of insurrections, resembles in some respects an account of the Crusades of old. The part played by the press in demanding intervention in the island offers abundant material for a study in war propaganda.

In discussions of the causes of the Spanish-American War, historians have made only passing reference to the influence of the "yellow journals." To state merely that these journals were active in behalf of the Cuban rebels is to tell only a part of the story. Their influence was much more far-reaching than appears on the surface, for their activity in exploiting the Cuban revolt and in selling their news services to other newspapers made it possible for all parts of the country to get partisan accounts of the Cuban insurrection.

Though this study is an indictment of the war-mongering press, it serves also to show the great power of newspapers when they work together in fostering international hatred and distrust. In the same way, the united efforts of an enlightened press would prove tremendously effective in creating the conditions of world peace and a better understanding among all nations.

Most of the material for this study was obtained from newspaper files though much information was gathered from periodicals. Some of the documents, particularly the *Congressional Record,* have been examined to supplement the newspapers and to check the accuracy of statements made by them. Additional checks were made also to determine the truth of certain newspaper statements concerning filibustering expeditions and belligerency rights.

The author realizes the problems involved in attempting to present an accurate measure of public opinion, but he believes that he has given sufficient evidence in the following pages to show that the American press played a large part in leading the United States into a war with Spain.

The writer wishes to make grateful acknowledgment to Professor Willard Grosvenor Bleyer, Director of the School of Journalism at the University of Wisconsin, at whose suggestion this work was undertaken and whose helpful advice has proved invaluable in the writing of this study; to Professor Frederic L. Paxson, Chairman of the History Department at the University of Wisconsin, who patiently guided the author through two years of research and whose sound scholarship was always an inspiration; to Ralph O. Nafziger,

Assistant Professor of Journalism at the University of Wisconsin, who offered many vaulable suggestions; to Professor Charles W. Pipkin, Dean of the Graduate School at Louisiana State University, whose practical advice and aid have made possible the publication of this work; to Professor Marvin G. Osborn, Director of the School of Journalism at Louisiana State University, who read the manuscript and made many practical suggestions; and to Taylor Cole, Associate Professor of Government at Louisiana State University, for his kindly criticism.

To his wife, Helen Crowell Wilkerson, whose critical judgment and assistance were of inestimable value, the writer wishes to express his deepest gratitude.

M.M.W.

Louisiana State University
Baton Rouge, Louisiana
October 18, 1932.

CHAPTER I

NEWS SERVICES AND SPECIAL CORRESPONDENTS

In a study of newspaper influence in relation to war propaganda, several difficult problems arise, one of which is a determination of the source and accuracy of news reports. In the three-year period preceding the outbreak of the Spanish-American War, a group of American newspapers were actively engaged in exploiting the Cuban revolt against Spanish rule and in advocating the cause of the rebels, some to build circulation and acquire prestige, others because they sincerely felt that the revolutions were contests for democracy and that the Cubans should be granted self-government. How news of the final insurrection, which broke out in February, 1895, was secured by the press in the face of Spanish opposition and at the cost of accuracy and distributed to all parts of the United States forms an important chapter in the study of public opinion and the conflict with Spain.

At the outbreak of the revolt there were in the United States two large news gathering associations, the Western Associated Press and the United Press (old), of which most of the larger newspapers were members.[1] For several years there had been much rivalry between these two organizations and by 1895 this feeling had grown intense. After the Western Associated Press had arranged an alliance with Reuter's Agency, a European news gathering association, the United Press declined in prestige and in 1897 it became insolvent and passed out of existence,[2] upon which most of its members joined the Associated Press.[3] Thus in 1895, most of the daily newspapers held membership in one of the several news gathering organizations and after 1897, the majority of the daily newspapers of the country were members of the Associated Press.[4]

---

1 Melville E. Stone, "The Associated Press" in *Century Magazine* XLVIII, June, 1905, 306. The United Press was in no sense connected historically to the United Press of the present day.

2 *Ibid.*, 307.

3 It was not until 1900, however, that the present Associated Press was organized.

4 *"M. E. S." His Book—A Tribute and a Souvenir to the Twenty-five Years, 1893-1918, of the Service of Melville E. Stone as General Manager of the Associated Press* (New York, 1928), 32.

Newspaper propaganda for the Cuban rebels centered about several New York newspapers, notably the *World* and *Journal,* both of which sent their best correspondents to the island.[5] The *Sun* and *Herald* also had special writers in Cuba.[6] Among the well known correspondents who covered the revolt for the *World* were Dr. William Shaw Bowen, Sylvester Scovel, W. W. Gay, James Creelman, and the woman writer, Cecil Charles. Creelman, however, joined the *Journal* staff during the latter part of 1896. The Hearst paper sent to the island Frederick W. Lawrence, Richard Harding Davis and several other reporters, and also the "artist," Frederic Remington.

These New York publications sold their news services, including pictures, to papers in all parts of the country. The Chicago *Tribune* used the New York *World* service,[7] and also the New York *Journal* syndicate service.[8] The Boston *Herald*[9] and the Chicago *Times-Herald* secured the New York *Herald* service,[10] and the San Francisco *Chronicle* took both the New York *Herald* and the *Sun* services.[11] The San Francisco *Examiner,* a Hearst paper, was furnished the same news service as the New York *Journal.* The Milwaukee *Sentinel* obtained its news of the Cuban revolt from the Washington *Post,*[12] while the New Orleans *Times-Democrat,* during the early part of the revolt, had its own correspondent in Havana,[13] and later it received the New York *Sun* news service.[14] Most of these newspapers after 1897 also utilized the Associated Press reports.[15]

The invasion of Cuba by the New York newspapers led the Associated Press to maintain a staff of men at strategic centers in the island and news "was smuggled out by the A.P. men at the imminent risk of being shot for their pains."[16] According to their by-laws, press associations had the right to use news matter secured by member papers, and the Associated Press frequently exercised this right by transmitting

[5] Chicago *Tribune,* Feb. 6, 1897, 1.
[6] Boston *Herald,* April 18, 1897, 1.
[7] Chicago *Tribune,* March 8, 1896, 2.
[8] *Ibid.,* Feb. 21, 1897, 1.
[9] Boston *Herald,* April 18, 1897, 1.
[10] Chicago *Times-Herald,* April 26, 1898, 6.
[11] San Francisco *Chronicle,* May 11, 1896, 1.
[12] Milwaukee *Sentinel,* April 12, 1898, 2.
[13] New Orleans *Times-Democrat,* March 8, 1895, 1. The *Times-Democrat* was merged with the New Orleans *Picayune* in 1914, the result of the merger being the present *Times-Picayune.*
[14] *Ibid.,* Feb. 9, 1898, 1.
[15] *Associated Press Reports,* 1895, 44-55; 1897, 38-47.
[16] *"M. E. S." His Book, op. cit.,* 159-160.

news stories taken from dispatches written by special correspondents in Cuba.[17]

The *World* by 1895 had become a member of the Western Associated Press,[18] and the New York *Herald,* the New York *Times,* and the New York *Tribune* joined the association in 1897.[19] The New York *Journal* was denied membership, largely because of the opposition of the *World* with which it was engaged in a bitter contest for supremacy in New York, but in 1897 it secured an Associated Press franchise for the *Morning Journal* through the purchase of a member paper, the *Commercial Advertiser,* with which it united. Thus by 1897 virtually all of the important New York newspapers, except the *Sun* which did not become a member of the A.P. until 1916, were members of a strong co-operative news gathering organization, and their news became available to the association for transmission to other member papers. When these New York publications sent correspondents to Cuba there was made available to nearly every paper in the country through the Associated Press as much news of the Cuban insurrection as was available to the New York press.

The syndicate service of New York newspapers offered a more complete coverage of the insurrection than could be obtained through the Associated Press. The fact that such service included illustrations was an important item in presenting a full picture of Spanish atrocities.[20]

Throughout the period of the Cuban insurrection there was much rivalry among the newspapers of Boston, New York, Chicago, and San Francisco. Especially was the contest bitter between the *World* and *Journal,* which had developed into a fight for supremacy in the field of New York journalism conducted by Joseph Pulitzer and William Randolph Hearst. Pulitzer bought the *World* in 1883 and by launching an aggressive editorial policy and adding typographical innovations to his paper had built a small, insignificant publication into one of the most influential papers in New York. Beginning with a circulation of some 15,000, the *World,* under Pulitzer, had reached by April, 1896, a circulation of 742,673 a day.[21]

---

[17] *Cf.* New Orleans *Times-Democrat,* May 11, 1896, 1; *ibid.,* Feb. 2, 1897, 2; *ibid.,* Feb. 8, 1897, 2; Indianapolis *Journal,* Feb. 6, 1897, 5.
[18] *Associated Press Reports,* 1895, 44-55.
[19] *Ibid.,* 1897, 38-47.
[20] Chicago *Tribune,* Feb. 2, 1897, 1.
[21] *World,* May 1, 1896, 1.

Hearst, who had great wealth at his disposal, entered New York journalism with his purchase of the *Morning Journal* in 1895, and soon became the most formidable rival Pulitzer had ever encountered. After the *Journal* as a one-cent paper had reached a circulation early in 1896 of 150,000, the *World* reduced its price to that of its competitor.[22] The two papers continued to grow rapidly in circulation and by early 1898 both had exceeded the 800,000 mark.[23]

On the Pacific coast, the San Francisco *Examiner,* like the *Journal,* was setting the pace in the practice of giving striking display to news which the *Chronicle* was striving to follow.[24] This competition led to much controversy between the two rivals.

The competition of the *World* and *Journal,* which were rushing special editions on early trains to Boston, was causing grave concern to the Boston *Herald.*[25] These two New York newspapers, with their sensational display of news, particularly of the Cuban revolt, were evidently making inroads into the *Herald* circulation. There was also a fight for circulation in Chicago between the *Tribune* and the *Times-Herald.*[26]

During this period the New York newspapers, following the lead of the *World* and *Journal,* introduced many innovations in gathering news, especially of the Cuban rebellion. Referring to these innovations, Walter L. Hawley of the New York *Evening Sun* wrote:[27]

> Today the hiring of special trains, the stringing of a special line of telegraph wire, the charter of a ship, the fitting out of an exploring expedition, or any other great innovation in the way of collecting information for the newspapers of the United States, is so much a part of the every day business of journalism that such things are accepted as a matter of course, or cause no more than passing comment.

Spanish authorities, soon after the outbreak of the insurrection, placed a strict censorship over all news emanat-

---

[22] *Ibid.,* Feb. 10, 1896, 1.
[23] *Cf. ibid.,* April 3, 1898, 6; *Journal,* April 4, 1898, 6.
[24] *Chronicle,* May 18, 1896, 6.
[25] Boston *Herald,* March 3, 1898, 6.
[26] *Times-Herald,* Jan. 25, 1898, 6.
[27] Walter L. Hawley, "Development of the American Newspaper" in *Popular Science Monthly,* LVI, December, 1899, 203.

ing from Cuba.[28] Whether or not this was done as a military measure or because the Spanish government feared publicity, as was suggested by Cuban sympathizers, can only be conjectured.[29] It is true, however, that the correspondents had a difficult time getting news of the revolt.[30] The insurrection was confined primarily to the least accessible provinces of the island. Much of the fighting was carried on by small bands in guerrilla fashion and this aggravated the natural obstacles encountered in obtaining accurate news.[31] To complicate the problems of the correspondents in obtaining news, the Spanish authorities restricted the passage of reporters beyond the lines of the Spanish troops and forbade communication with the enemy, thus cutting off whatever connection that might have been maintained openly with rebel bands.[32] It was charged that many of the correspondents established headquarters at Key West where they wrote "news" dispatches based on rumors and unconfirmed reports received from the Cuban Junta.[33] Some of the reporters, however, stated that they kept up communication with the rebels by secret means.

This restriction of news caused much friction between newspaper correspondents and the Spanish military authorities, and contributed materially to the stirring up of opposition in the United States against the Spaniards. Naturally the correspondents objected to having their dispatches censored, and they evaded the censorship order whenever they could.[34] In doing so they had to smuggle their news aboard vessels bound for Key West to be transmitted to their papers by telegraph. Referring to the difficulty encountered in obtaining news of the revolt, one writer said that "transmitting news to New York by surreptitious means were efforts which taxed the courage and ingenuity of the best trained men."[35] In this manner was the censorship problem solved to the liking of the New York editors, but such violation of the Spanish order only embittered the Spaniards toward the Americans in general and the correspondents in particular.

---

[28] New York *Times*, March 6, 1895, 5.
[29] *Ibid.*, Aug. 7, 1895, 4.
[30] *Ibid.*, March 6, 1895, 5.
[31] *Ibid.*, July 4, 1895, 5.
[32] *World*, Feb. 17, 1896, 1.
[33] *Times-Herald*, Feb. 19, 1896, 6.
[34] "*M. E. S.*" *His Book, op. cit.*, 159-160.
[35] *Ibid.*, 159.

But the problem of passing the Spanish lines was not so easily solved. It was comparatively easy for the Spaniards to control communications with the area in revolt, and correspondents found it difficult to obtain news. One reason for Spain's refusal to allow American journalists passage through their lines was the fear that the correspondents were negotiating the sale of arms and ammunition to the rebels.[36] Some of the bolder correspondents attempted to establish communication with the Cubans, among whom was one Charles Govin, a Florida correspondent, who succeeded in passing the patrols, but was later captured and executed.[37] Another correspondent attempting to reach the rebel lines was Sylvester Scovel of the *World*.[38] Scovel was arrested, and for days his case was presented to the American public through the press and from the platform, in legislative hall and in the school room as exemplifying martyrdom to the cause of freedom of speech and the press.

The *World* made an appeal to the country at large insisting that its correspondent be accorded all the rights of an American citizen.[39] The case was carried to Congress when the Secretary of State was requested by the Senate to present to Spain the imperative necessity of bringing Scovel to Havana and "to insist that he shall have all the rights guaranteed by treaty to American citizens."[40]

The *World* made the most of its opportunity in "playing up" the case of Scovel. Through news story and editorial, it followed the prisoner, carrying a paragraph daily at the beginning of its editorial page which gave the number of days Scovel had lain in prison.[41] Senator Morgan of Alabama, a Cuban sympathizer, in the Senate denounced the administration for not securing the release of the correspondent,[42] after which the Pulitzer paper asserted that the "life and liberty of American citizens abroad will be protected at any cost."[43] Finally, the *World* announced that through "the quick work of John Sherman (Secretary of State)" Scovel was to be released without trial.[44]

[36] New York *Times*, May 6, 1895, 5.
[37] *World*, Jan. 7, 1897, 7.
[38] *Ibid.*, Feb. 7, 1897, 1.
[39] *Ibid.*, Jan. 7, 1897, 7.
[40] *Ibid.*, Feb. 13, 1897, 1.
[41] *Ibid.*, Feb. 25, 1897, 6.
[42] *Ibid.*, Feb. 13, 1897, 1.
[43] *Ibid.*, Feb. 23, 1897, 1.
[44] *Ibid.*, March 10, 1897, 1.

Other papers throughout the country published accounts of Scovel's arrest furnished by the Associated Press.[45] The Chicago *Tribune,* which used the *World* news service, carried the same accounts of the case as did the *World.*[46] The Scovel case brought editorial comments from several newspapers in widely separated sections of the country. The Indianapolis *Journal* stated that "his arrest was wholly without justification" and his imprisonment was an insult to the American flag,[47] and the Chicago *Tribune,* referring to Scovel's arrest as proof of Spain's desire to prevent knowledge of her cruel treatment of the rebels, asserted that "the outside world may easily infer that the rest of the big island is a seething volcano of insurrection."[48]

That the agitation of Scovel's case in the newspapers had the effect of attracting the attention of the public to conditions in Cuba is seen in the action taken to secure his release. A mass meeting was held in Dallas, Texas, in protest against his arrest, at which resolutions were adopted calling on the Texas senators and representatives to bring the matter before Congress with the view of effecting Scovel's release.[49] The legislatures of New York, New Jersey, Pennsylvania, Indiana, North Carolina,[50] Illinois, Nebraska,[51] Arkansas, Minnesota, Iowa, and Massachusetts took action to secure his release,[52] and a resolution was introduced in the United States Senate requesting the Secretary of State to use his good offices with the Spanish government in behalf of Scovel.[53] A few days later the *World* announced that the "pulpit takes up Scovel's cause,"[54] and that "the alumni of the University of Michigan pledge themselves to strive for the release of the *World* correspondent."[55]

Richard Harding Davis, in writing about Scovel's arrest, said that "his imprisonment is an affront to the laws of the nations and an outrage upon the liberty of an American citizen."[56] During his imprisonment Scovel continued to write

---

45 *Times-Democrat,* Feb. 8, 1897, 2; Indianapolis *Journal,* Feb. 8, 1897, 1; *ibid.,* Feb. 20, 1897, 6; San Francisco *Chronicle,* Feb. 9, 1897, 6; Milwaukee *Sentinel,* Feb. 8, 1897, 2.
46 Chicago *Tribune,* Feb. 7, 1897, 1.
47 Indianapolis *Journal,* Feb. 20, 1897, 6.
48 Chicago *Tribune,* Feb. 28, 1897, 6.
49 *World,* Feb. 15, 1897, 7.
50 *Ibid.,* Feb. 17, 1897, 1.
51 *Ibid.,* Feb. 19, 1897, 1.
52 *Ibid.,* Feb. 21, 1897, 1.
53 *Congressional Record,* 54 Congress, 2 Session, XXIX, Pt. 2, 1762, Feb. 12, 1897.
54 *World,* Feb. 24, 1897, 6.
55 *Ibid.,* Feb. 22, 1897, 2.
56 *Ibid.,* Feb. 23, 1897, 1.

for the *World,* secretly dispatching his news each day, and the newspaper's circulation increased more than 8,000 during his confinement.[57] In this connection, the Pulitzer paper boasted that it addressed more persons each Sunday than all of the ministers in the state of New York combined.[58]

Two other *World* correspondents, Creelman and Gay, were expelled from Cuba for "telling the truth about Weyler."[59] Creelman, who had been writing atrocity stories for the *World* when he was ordered to leave the island by Captain-General Weyler, was considered one of the best of the *World's* staff writers. Commenting editorially on his expulsion, the *World* said:[60]

> The expulsion of Mr. Creelman puts the Spanish attempt to suppress the Cuban revolution in its true light, as an appeal to cruelty, an affront at extermination and a relapse into ferocity and barbarism which marked the original conquests of Spain on this continent.

Frederick W. Lawrence, correspondent for the New York *Journal,* was expelled with Creelman by Weyler,[61] and Thomas Robinson Hawley, Jr., "artist for a New York newspaper," was imprisoned for the eighth time within one month for attempting to send out pictures of the Cuban revolt to the United States.[62] Later, another *Journal* correspondent and a reporter for the New York *Sun* were driven out of Cuba.[63] The *Journal* asserted that its representative was "ordered out of Cuba for telling the truth."[64] It also reported that Dupuy De Lome, the Spanish Minister at Washington, had sent Pinkerton agents to Havana to shadow newspapermen "to see that their correspondence is not biased."[65]

Another case of the arrest of a Cuban correspondent which attracted nation-wide comment was that of Ona Melton, a Jacksonville, Florida, correspondent.[66] Melton was taken prisoner aboard the "Competitor," a filibustering vessel captured by the Spaniards, tried with four others by court-

[57] *Ibid.,* Feb. 20, 1897, 1.
[58] *Ibid.,* March 15, 1897, 6.
[59] *Ibid.,* May 7, 1896, 1; *ibid.,* June 26, 1896, 7.
[60] *Ibid.,* May 7, 1896, 6.
[61] Chicago *Tribune,* May 7, 1896, 2.
[62] *World,* June 11, 1896, 7.
[63] *Journal,* Aug. 3, 1897, 2.
[64] *Ibid.,* Aug. 4, 1897, 6.
[65] *Ibid.,* March 15, 1897, 3.
[66] *World,* March 22, 1897, 6.

martial, and sentenced to be shot.[67] His execution was delayed, however, pending a new trial and for months he lay in prison awaiting disposition of his case.[68]

The New York *Journal,* which did not "play up" the arrest of Scovel because he was the correspondent of its competitor, the *World,* announced that it intended to "free Melton."[69] His incarceration, it stated, was "a typical instance of the contempt in which American citizenship had been held by Captain-General Weyler, under the permission of Grover Cleveland."[70] The Hearst paper added that the publicity given Melton's case caused the State Department to make formal demand for his release.[71]

During the early part of his imprisonment, Melton had written for the *World,* secretly dispatching his news articles to this country, one of which was displayed with the words: "Horrors of 19 Months in a Spanish Dungeon; Melton's Tale of Spanish Cruelty."[72]

Notwithstanding the expulsion of correspondents from Cuba, the New York papers continued to receive full reports of the rebellion.[73]

This controversy between the newspapers and Spanish authorities over the rights of correspondents continued during the period of the revolt, with the former contending that its representatives should be unmolested and unrestricted in the gathering of news in Cuba and the latter insisting upon exercising a strict control over the movements of the newspapermen and the dispatches they sent out.

The Spanish government, in attempting to censor news of the insurrection, not only antagonized the correspondents but encouraged inaccuracy. The task of securing accurate reports of the revolt presented almost insurmountable obstacles without censorship because of the character of the fighting and the lack of adequate communications; with censorship it was reasonable to expect that writers would stoop to any means necessary to obtain news stories. The fact that the New York press continued to receive accounts of the Cuban rebellion after the correspondents had been expelled

---

[67] *Journal,* April 12, 1897, 1.
[68] *Ibid.,* April 13, 1897, 10.
[69] *Ibid.,* April 15, 1897, 1.
[70] *Ibid.,* April 4, 1897, 1.
[71] *Ibid.,* April 13, 1897, 10.
[72] *World,* Nov. 1, 1896, 1.
[73] *Cf. World, Journal, Sun,* and *Herald,* November and December, 1897.

from the island shows conclusively that the journalists were not obtaining their news reports from first-hand investigation. From what sources they secured "news" can only be conjectured—from travelers returning from the island, from seamen, from rumors emanating from the Florida coast, and bits of gossip picked up here and there. From whatever source their news came, it is improbable that it was accurate or even approached the truth.

It can be seen, therefore, how a few aggressive papers made available to the co-operative news gathering associations, through their special Cuban correspondents, unconfirmed "news" reports dealing with the activities of the rebels, which were in turn transmitted to every section of the United States. Through the persistence of these correspondents in seeking news in violation of Spanish orders, the Cuban question was further agitated in this country, and the Spanish government presented in the light of infringing upon the inalienable rights of American citizens. Thus was the groundwork laid for an effective campaign for the Cuban cause.

CHAPTER II

FILIBUSTERING AND SENSATIONAL JOURNALISM

The fitting out of filibustering expeditions in the United States to aid the Cubans raised one of the most serious controversies between this government and Spain that came up during the revolution. Filibustering had been carried on from the United States with every Cuban revolt since 1823, in violation of the neutrality laws of this country. Before the outbreak of the revolution, influential Cuban leaders had organized in this country the Junta, an organization composed of naturalized and unnaturalized Cubans and Cuban sympathizers, the purposes of which were to raise money to aid the Cuban cause, to promote the fitting out of filibustering expeditions, and to arouse sympathy among Americans for the rebels. Many Cubans also came to this country, took out naturalization papers, and, protected by American citizenship, returned to the island to aid the rebels.[1] The activities of the Junta and the naturalized Cubans in the service of the provisional Cuban government caused serious entanglements with Spain.

It was through the efforts of the Junta, aided by sympathizers, that filibustering expeditions were fitted out from American ports. In the early part of the revolt, these expeditions sailed openly, moving President Cleveland in June, 1895, to issue a proclamation calling attention to the neutrality acts and admonishing all citizens of the United States to refrain from engaging in any enterprise that might involve this country in a controversy with a friendly power.[2] The President's proclamation, however, apparently served no purpose other than to place the administration on record as to its neutrality stand.[3]

Upon repeated complaints from Spain, authorities of the United States made efforts to prevent the sailing of filibustering expeditions and to effect their capture if they succeeded in escaping from American ports.[4] Coast guard cutters,

[1] James D. Richardson, *A Compilation of the Messages and Papers of the Presidents* (Washington, 1898), IX, 718.
[2] New York *Times*, June 13, 1895, 5.
[3] *Ibid.*, Sept. 25, 1895, 5.
[4] *Ibid.*, June 14, 1895, 5.

therefore, were sent to the Florida coast, the many small bays and inlets of which made it an ideal place for filibustering activities, to guard against the unlawful sailing of vessels.[5] In his fourth message to Congress, President Cleveland, in discussing the Cuban question, referred to the difficulty of policing effectively the long coast line of this country against unlawful expeditions, giving the impression that the United States had exercised "due diligence" in trying to prevent the sailing of filibusters.[6] He further stated that the Cubans in this country were promoting the insurrection through the press, by public meetings, by the purchase and shipment of arms, by the raising of funds and other means "which the spirit of our institutions and the tenor of our laws do not permit to be made the subject of criminal prosecution."[7] The term "due diligence" is indefinite, and what this government regarded as diligence in guarding its coast, Spanish authorities tended to look upon as half-hearted efforts.[8] In consequence, the Spanish government dispatched vessels to cruise near the Florida coast,[9] which action was regarded as an "invasion" by the people of Key West and further embittered Americans against the Spaniards.[10]

On the whole, the authorities of the United States were fairly successful in stopping filibusters. During the insurrection, seventy-one expeditions were fitted out from the United States and of this number, only twenty-seven were landed in Cuba, most of the remainder having been halted by the United States. There were some thirty-one separate vessels engaged, more or less constantly, in the service of the Cubans.

The failure of the government of the United States to secure convictions of filibusters captured by American vessels tended to encourage activities, and it was not until early in 1898 that a favorable court decision was handed down which made it difficult to evade the law.

The activities of the Spanish government in attempting to stop filibusters resulted in sharp diplomatic controversies with this country, which were aggravated by the manner in which the news reports were handled by a part of the Ameri-

[5] *World,* July 29, 1895, 7.
[6] Richardson, *op. cit.,* IX, 719.
[7] *Ibid.,* IX, 718.
[8] New York *Times,* June 10, 1895, 5.
[9] *World,* June 10, 1895, 5.
[10] New York *Times,* Sept. 18, 1895, 5.

can press. One of the first and most serious instances of this kind was the "Allianca" affair, which occurred in March, 1895. The "Allianca" was an American steamship on its homeward voyage from Colon to New York, when six miles from the coast of Cuba, off Cape Maysi, it was signalled to "heave to" by the Spanish gunboat "Conde De Venadito."[11] The "Allianca" refused to halt whereupon the Spanish vessel gave chase and then fired upon the "Allianca" repeatedly.[12] The Spanish authorities claimed that the American vessel was in the act of transferring munitions of war to fishing vessels to be transported to the Cuban shore for the use of the rebels, but the Captain of the "Allianca" denied this. The Commander of the Spanish vessel contended that the "Allianca" was within the three-mile zone of the Cuban coast, a charge which was also denied by the American Captain.[13] The State Department held that the Windward Passage, where the incident occurred, was the natural highway for vessels plying between ports of the United States and the Caribbean sea, and that forcible intervention with them "can not be claimed as a belligerent act, whether they pass within three miles of the Cuban coast or not and can under no circumstances be tolerated when no state of war exists."[14]

The point at issue was a complicated one. Under the rules of international law, Spain had no legal right of visitation and search upon the high seas inasmuch as she had not recognized that a state of war existed in Cuba. This question had arisen on several occasions during the "Ten Years' War" when Spain had captured vessels flying the American flag on the high seas, and each time the Spanish government was required to make reparations. On the other hand, Spain could legally exercise police powers within her territorial waters, extending three miles from the coast line. Ordinarily, if the "Allianca" was within the three-mile zone, the Spanish authorities would have been justified in accosting the vessel and, upon its refusal to "heave to," in giving chase upon the high seas. The State Department of the United States, however, argued that under the circumstances foreign vessels had the right to pass unmolested through Windward Passage re-

[11] *Foreign Relations*, 1895, II, 1177, telegram from Gresham, Secretary of State, to Taylor, Minister to Spain, March 14, 1895.
[12] *Idem.*
[13] *World*, March 13, 1895, 1.
[14] *Foreign Relations*, 1895, II, 1177, Gresham to Taylor, March 14, 1895.

gardless of proximity to the Cuban coast. A sharp note was dispatched to Madrid asking for a full explanation of the conduct of the Spanish Captain.[15]

Meanwhile, American newspapers in every section of the country came out with the striking headline, "Our Flag Fired On." The news report in the *World* stated that "a steamship belonging to the United States, carrying the United States mail, and flying the American flag was fired on, apparently without provocation or justification, by a Spanish gunboat when on the high seas off Cuba.'"[16] Referring to the incident editorially, the *World* said that the American flag had been insulted on the high seas and the lives and property of American citizens had been endangered by the recklessness of "a stupid commander" of the Spanish navy.[17]

The New York *Sun* argued with a degree of truth that the "Allianca" was running from one neutral port to another in time of peace when she was fired on without provocation.[18] Editorially, the *Sun* referred to the affair in these words:[19]

> It is evident that the Spanish government whose arrogance and brutality provoke its Cuban subjects to rebellion, requires a sharp and stinging lesson at the hands of the United States. . . . The American flag has been insulted and the lives and property of American citizens have been placed in jeopardy. The next vessel ought to be pursued and blown out of the water. Let it (the State Department) bring Spain to her knees, or punish her by the destruction of her navy and the loss of Cuba.

For several days following the incident, the *Sun* carried two columns daily concerning the event, while negotiations were being conducted by the two countries with the view of peacefully settling the question.[20] William C. Whitney, former Secretary of the Navy, was quoted as saying that it was a case of a willful insult to the American flag and people,[21] and Dana's paper asked if Cleveland meant "to knuckle to Spain," adding that it made no difference "if the 'Allianca'

---

[15] Chicago *Tribune,* May 12, 1895, 6.
[16] *World,* March 13, 1895, 1.
[17] *Ibid.,* 4.
[18] *Sun,* March 13, 1895, 1.
[19] *Ibid.,* March 14, 1895, 6.
[20] *Cf. ibid.,* March 14-16, 1895, 1.
[21] *Ibid.,* March 19, 1895, 1.

was within the three-mile zone of Cuba that was no reason for firing on the American flag.'"[22] The newspaper stated that "whatever turn the 'Allianca' affair may take, and whatever decision in regard to it may be reached by the State Department, our naval forces in the Gulf do not mean to be caught napping.'"[23]

The Chicago *Tribune* asserted that the "Allianca" incident was not the first in which "outrages of this sort have been committed by the hot-blooded Spaniards, but it is high time they should be stopped."[24] The Milwaukee *Sentinel* stated that "this hostile and insolent act was committed under circumstances that offer no excuses whatever for its occurrences," and that the "tendency to support Cuba's desire for independence is incalculably strengthened in this country by the late indignity offered our flag."[25] The San Francisco *Chronicle* carried a special dispatch from New York of the "Allianca" affair, referring editorially to the incident as "a manifest outrage on the American flag."[26]

Both the Indianapolis *Journal*[27] and the Cincinnati *Commercial-Gazette* referred to the "Allianca" affair as "an insult to Old Glory."[28] In discussing the incident editorially, the *Commercial-Gazette* remarked:[29]

> Once more a Spanish war vessel has fired upon an American ship, but what of it? That's a little bit of fun Spanish ships have been indulging in every now and then for the last 40 years. It has got to be so common that our authorities at Washington never trouble themselves about it.

The Chicago *Times-Herald* stated that not only had the "Allianca" been fired on but "if reports be true, other boats carrying the Stars and Stripes have fared no better,"[30] and the Boston *Herald* called the incident a "willful insult to our flag."[31]

---

[22] *Ibid.*, March 22, 1895, 6.
[23] *Ibid.*, March 24, 1895, 6.
[24] Chicago *Tribune*, March 16, 1895, 12.
[25] *Sentinel*, March 16, 1895, 4.
[26] *Chronicle*, March 14, 1895, 6.
[27] Indianapolis *Journal*, March 13, 1895, 5.
[28] *Commercial-Gazette*, March 13, 1895, 1.
[29] *Ibid.*, March 15, 1895, 4.
[30] *Times-Herald*, March 19, 1895, 5.
[31] Boston *Herald*, March 19, 1895, 1.

The New York *Times* was quite as severe as the *Herald* in its condemnation of "the insult."[32] For several days it ran editorial comment picturing the Spanish officers as "haughty and irresponsible beings." It said that "a deal of sturdy lying is to be expected from the commander of the Spanish gunboat," and that "some time one of these gentlemen of Spain will get into the most serious difficulty of his life through this habit of overhauling American vessels and our first news of the affair will be that it is all settled."[33]

A reader of the New York *Herald* was much wrought up over the incident:[34]

> Old Glory must not be so outrageously insulted like this by any foreign nation. If our government asks the Spanish government for an ample apology and does not receive it, then it is for the U.S. to telegraph to Admiral Meade's fleet to proceed at once to Cuba and destroy her, and in return go to Spain and let her smell a little of our Yankee smokeless powder.

The Associated Press carried an account of the incident, which was used by member papers with conspicuous display. Thus those newspapers which were unable to maintain correspondents in Cuba were furnished reports of the episode.[35]

Leslie's Weekly saw in the incident an opportunity for the United States to use a warship to create respect for American rights, asserting that Spain would apologize because "we could overmatch her easily, ship for ship, and with her lack of money she would hesitate to enter into a combat with us."[36]

The "Allianca" incident was settled to the satisfaction of the United States when Spain admitted that the American vessel was outside Spanish waters and disavowed the course pursued by the Captain of the "Venadito."

The second serious incident arising out of filibustering activities, which aroused the indignation of the American press and for a time caused strained diplomatic relations between Spain and this country, was the "Competitor" affair,

---

[32] New York *Times,* March 13, 1895, 4.
[33] *Idem.*
[34] New York *Herald,* March 16, 1895, 3.
[35] *Cf.* New Orleans *Times-Democrat,* March 14, 1895, 2.
[36] *Leslie's Weekly,* LXXX, April 4, 1895, 15.

which occurred in May, 1896. The "Competitor" was a small schooner operating between the United States and Cuba.[37] It was captured either on the high seas or within the three-mile zone of Cuba, and its crew of five men taken prisoners, tried by court-martial, and sentenced to be shot.[38] Two of the prisoners, including Ona Melton, were citizens of the United States and one was an English subject.[39] Immediately a strong protest came from the newspapers against the method by which the men were tried and the sentence imposed.

The Chicago *Tribune* contended that the crew were tried by secret court-martial in violation of the Protocol of 1877 with Spain.[40] This Protocol stipulated that American prisoners accused of hostile acts against the Spanish government should have open trial; that copies of the charges against them should be furnished; and that they should have counsel and witnesses and be supplied with the evidence and names of witnesses summoned by the prosecution. In its contention the *Tribune* was correct unless Spain could show that the crew had been captured with "arms in hand" within the three-mile zone of the Cuban coast.[41]

The *Tribune,* however, misrepresented the facts when it stated that if the vessel were captured on the high seas Spain had violated the treaty and "if it was captured within the three-mile zone, Spain had violated the treaty in the manner of the trial."[42] The *Tribune* should have added that the manner in which the trial was conducted was a violation of the treaty unless Spain could show that the men were taken within the three-mile zone "with arms in hand." Contending that the "Competitor" was not in Cuban waters when it was captured, the *Tribune* advocated drastic action by the United States:[43]

> If the reports be correct that the ships of the Atlantic squadron are being hurriedly prepared for sea

[37] *World,* May 15, 1896, 1.
[38] Chicago *Tribune,* May 12, 1896, 6.
[39] *World,* May 15, 1896, 1.
[40] Chicago *Tribune,* May 12, 1896, 6.
[41] *Ibid.,* May 14, 1896, 6. The Protocol reads as follows: "No citizen of the U. S. residing in Spain, her adjacent islands, or her ultramarine possessions, charged with acts of sedition, treason or conspiracy against the institutions, the public security, the integrity of the territory, or against the supreme government, or any other crime whatsoever, shall not be subject to trial by any exceptional tribunal but exclusively by the ordinary jurisdiction except in the case of being captured with arms in hand".
[42] *Ibid.,* May 12, 1896, 6.
[43] *Ibid.,* May 10, 1896, 32.

duty and are about to go into commission it might be well to send a few down to Cuba and add the weight of cannon to the documentary evidence that Uncle Sam cannot be trifled with all the time.

The next day the *Tribune* carried a news article to the effect that "Spain is wild with rage" and that "there is a popular demand (in Spain) for the death of the filibusters."[44] The newspaper admitted, however, that evidence had not been submitted showing where the "Competitor" had been captured, but added that "whether it were captured on the high seas or within the three-mile limit of the Cuban coast matters little as touching the right of summary action by the Spanish authorities."[45] Urging that a fleet and troops be sent to Cuba, the *Tribune* contended that the United States should "sink every Spanish vessel there, knock Morro Castle to flinders, and march in and hold the city." There had been already too much "trifling and dilly-dallying," it continued, for the time had come "to notify insolent Spain that she must turn over a new leaf." It boasted that the "Lauredo" and "Three Friends," two filibustering vessels, "are prepared to fight if attacked by Spain."[46]

Asserting that "Uncle Sam has been defied" and that Weyler had "expressed his contempt for the United States," the *World* stated that the "Competitor" trial was a farce and that when the schooner's crew were captured "Old Glory was fired upon repeatedly." It also published a news article, written by Creelman, referring to the "Competitor" affair in these words:[47]

It is scarcely possible to imagine a more deliberate defiance of the United States than the so-called trial of the five prisoners captured on the American schooner, Competitor, before a summary naval court-martial yesterday. The court simply spat upon the treaty, and the solemn protests of Consul-General Williams were read to the judges by the Judicial secretary with a sneer. . . . If the two Americans—Laborde and Melton— and the Englishman, Gildea—are shot it will be murder.

[44] *Ibid.*, May 11, 1896, 2.
[45] *Ibid.*, 6.
[46] *Ibid.*, May 24, 1896, 2.
[47] *World*, May 15, 1896, 1.

Discussing the trial editorially, the *World* said:[48]

> The bombardment of the capitol at Washington would be no more an act of war than would have been the murder of American citizens under sentence of a prejudiced court-martial. Americans will never condone such a lawless butchery of their countrymen as was contemplated by Weyler's drumhead tribunal.

At this time, Senator Morgan of Alabama presented a resolution in the Senate directing the Committee on Foreign Relations to inquire into and report on the rights of citizens of the United States under the treaties with Spain with respect to the trial of those "now under sentence of death in Cuba."[49] Commenting on the resolution, the *World* stated that "every day of the confinement of the American prisoners at Havana is a day of American dishonor" and that "justice and honor are alike outraged by such a transaction."[50] Senator Morgan, in a speech in the Senate, advocated the sending of warships to Cuba to demand the release of the American prisoners.[51] The *World* was also in favor of quick action, asking if the United States should "let Weyler shoot these American citizens without trial, without proof of guilt, and under circumstances which go very strongly to show that in fact no offense was committed."[52]

Spain, yielding to the protests of the United States, agreed to reconsider the death sentences imposed upon the five prisoners, and the case was permitted to go to the Supreme Military and Naval Court of Appeals, but a hearing was postponed from time to time.[53] Discussing one of these delays, the *World* said:[54]

> The men thus deprived of their liberty without form of law were taken by violence from under the American flag after it had been fired on, and even if it is true that they were running the Spanish blockade, it is equally true that the blockade has not been officially established nor is it officially recognized by the United States or any other country. For the offense of attempting to

[48] *Ibid.*, 6.
[49] *Idem.*
[50] *Idem.*
[51] *Ibid.*, June 6, 1896, 7.
[52] *Idem.*
[53] *Ibid.*, May 12, 1896, 1.
[54] *Ibid.*, July 10, 1896, 6.

> deliver articles of merchandise which can become contraband of war only after belligerency has been recognized these American citizens are held under sentence of death from an illegal court-martial and month after month the civil trial to which they are entitled is denied them because it does not suit the political purposes of the Spanish administration to give it. What will American citizenship be worth if we do not maintain its dignity by insisting on its rights?

The *World* used cartoons frequently and effectively in arguing its point, one of which extended across four columns of its front page showing the American flag stretched from Florida to Cuba with these words: "Notice! No American Citizen Shall Be Put to Death Without a Fair Trial Before a Civil Tribunal."[55] When the date for the rehearing of the case of the prisoners was again delayed, the *World* grew indignant at "Spain's act of defiance."[56]

Whether the *World* was more interested in the welfare of the "Competitor" prisoners or its circulation is a matter for speculation. At any rate, its circulation for one week in June, 1896, after the trial of the crew, totaled 5,114,628, a gain over the same period in 1895 of some 216,823 per day.[57] The Cuban insurrection was proving a profitable conflict for the *World!*

Using the full news service of the New York *Herald,* the San Francisco *Chronicle* gave conspicuous display to the "Competitor" incident.[58] In connection with its news stories about the "Competitor" crew, the *Chronicle* carried illustrations showing "Spanish savagery 20 years ago" and "the butchery of the crew of the 'Virginius.' "[59] The "Virginius" incident had created indignation in this country in 1873 during the "Ten Years' War." The "Virginius" was an alleged filibustering vessel, flying the American flag and having an American registry. It was captured by the Spaniards after an eight-hour chase which began and ended on the high seas. The vessel was taken to Santiago, Cuba, where, after a summary trial by court-martial ostensibly on a charge of piracy, fifty-three of her crew and other persons on board,

[55] *Ibid.,* May 12, 1896, 1.
[56] *Ibid.,* Nov. 24, 1896, 1.
[57] *Ibid.,* June 14, 1896, 6.
[58] *Chronicle,* May 11, 1896, 1.
[59] *Ibid.,* May 12, 1896, 1.

including citizens of the United States, British subjects, and Cubans, were condemned to death and shot. The Spanish government contended that the "Virginius" was not entitled to carry the American flag and in this contention it was correct inasmuch as the vessel, while registered as the property of an American citizen, belonged to a Cuban rebel. It had on board men to be landed in Cuba, but Spain only had the right of seizing the ship within territorial waters. The case was settled after considerable negotiation upon the payment by Spain of $80,000 to the families of the executed Americans. The incident was not forgotten by the newspapers which referred to it repeatedly as typifying Spanish disregard for the rights of American citizens.

The *Chronicle* interpreted the "Competitor" incident as showing "the suddenness with which events turn in the direction of war."[60] After disavowing any intention on the part of the United States to annex Cuba, the *Chronicle* stated that "it is to Cuban liberty and autonomy that our sympathies tend; to Cuban hope and longing for free institutions."[61]

Referring to Spain's action in yielding to American demands for a re-hearing for the "Competitor" prisoners, the Washington *Post* asserted that "Spain averted an explosion of popular indignation in the United States which no administration, however pacifically inclined, could have resisted."[62] After stating that Weyler had threatened to resign his position unless the men were executed, the *Post* said:[63]

> Let us be frank. The Cuban insurgents have always had our sympathy, and in every private way our aid. It is nothing to be ashamed of from our point of view. It were idle and fatuous to look for peace and quiet so long as Spain holds Cuba in her relentless gripe (*sic*). There can be no security while Cuba bleeds.

The Boston *Herald* had received by mail the proceedings in the court-martial convened in Havana to try the "Competitor" crew.[64] The trial showed, the *Herald* stated, that the convictions "were the outcome of national prejudice."

---

[60] *Ibid.*, 6.
[61] *Ibid.*, May 15, 1896, 6.
[62] Washington *Post*, May 12, 1896, 1.
[63] *Ibid.*, May 18, 1896, 6.
[64] Boston *Herald*, May 11, 1896, 1.

The Chicago *Tribune,* however, had stated that the trial was held secretly and the records were therefore unavailable.[65]

The Indianapolis *Journal,* in criticizing Cleveland's foreign policy, stated that the "people are very tired of the administration's kid-glove manner in dealing with Spain and Cuban affairs, and especially of its failure to protect American citizenship."[66] If the Spanish authorities should refuse to be influenced by the protests of the President against summary execution of American citizens in violation of existing treaties, the *Journal* asserted, "Mr. Cleveland would not be doing his duty if he failed to use every means at his command to compel the Spanish authorities to respect our rights, even to the bombardment of Havana."[67]

The *Times-Democrat* was also outspoken in its opposition to the Spanish policy, referring to the "Competitor" incident in these words:[68]

> The Spaniards may fume and bluster as they please and may even indulge in the very innocent threat of sending a squadron this way and arming fast merchantmen to prey upon American commerce, (but) people will, as one man, approve the action of the United States government in interposing to prevent the rights of American citizens from being ridden roughshod over, even when American citizens have been doing what is wrong. . . . Success to them therefore (the Cubans); success, early and complete!

Another strong champion of the Cuban cause was the Charleston *News and Courier,* which argued that "it was bad enough for the people of this country to have to stand by and see Cuban captives murdered day after day" without having "citizens of the United States included in the ranks of the victims."[69] Quite as partisan as the *News and Courier* was the Chicago *Times-Herald,* which, in discussing the "Competitor" incident, asserted:[70]

> The Cuban question threatens to rise and torment this country again through the cross (*sic*) impertinence

65 Chicago *Tribune,* May 12, 1896, 6.
66 Indianapolis *Journal,* May 11, 1896, 4.
67 *Ibid.,* May 12, 1896, 4.
68 *Times-Democrat,* May 12, 1896, 4.
69 *News and Courier,* May 13, 1896, 4.
70 *Times-Herald,* May 11, 1896, 6.

> of Spanish officialism. The ghost of the "Virginius" crew arise to torture American statesmen, who venture to treat with the Spanish as with a highly civilized nation.

The Cincinnati *Commercial-Gazette* predicted that the "Competitor" case "may yet be the means of making Cuba free, even though Spain has called a halt."[71]

Contending that the "Competitor" was not carrying arms and that the crew were not armed, *Leslie's Weekly* asserted that Spain had no right to interfere with trade even within the three-mile zone.[72] The first part of this statement was in contradiction with one made by the Indianapolis *Journal*, which admitted that "there can be little doubt that the crew of the vessel alluded to were arrested under conditions which make it very certain that they were engaged in a hostile demonstration against Spain."[73] With reference to Spain's right to interfere with trade within the three-mile zone, *Leslie's Weekly* was misrepresenting facts if by "trade" it meant traffic in arms and ammunition. If the "Competitor" was carrying arms and ammunition, Spain had a legal right to protect her coast within the three-mile zone, regardless of whether or not the crew or passengers were armed.

After remaining in prison for more than eighteen months, the "Competitor" crew were pardoned by the Queen Regent of Spain, and this issue, which had been agitated by the press for months, came to a peaceful end.[74] Spain was apparently doing all she could to remove grounds for irritation on the part of the United States.[75]

While the case of the "Competitor" crew was pending, there were other filibustering expeditions which brought about controversies. Hardly a day passed during the early part of 1897 that the press did not carry stories of expeditions being fitted out.[76] Chief among these filibustering vessels was the "Three Friends," which had several encounters with Spanish gunboats in trying to land on the coast of Cuba.[77] The tugboat, "George W. Childs," was another which completed several voyages to Cuba.[78] The "Commo-

---

[71] *Commercial-Gazette*, May 12, 1897, 1.
[72] *Leslie's Weekly*, LXXXII, May 28, 1896, 25.
[73] Indianapolis *Journal*, Nov. 20, 1897, 4.
[74] *World*, Nov. 19, 1897, 1.
[75] Boston *Herald*, Nov. 19, 1897, 6.
[76] *Cf.* New York *Journal*, January, February, March, and April, 1897.
[77] *Ibid.*, Jan. 2, 1897, 1.
[78] *World*, June 14, 1895, 1; *ibid.*, June 17, 1895, 5; *ibid.*, July 4, 1895, 5.

dore," which sank off the Florida coast because of being overloaded but which the New York *Journal* said was "scuttled by a traitor,"[79] the "Dauntless,"[80] and the "Silver Heels" were other well known vessels in the service of the rebels.[81] The "Three Friends" was highly successful in its activities, and by the middle of 1897 it had more than cleared its costs in trips to Cuba and given proof of "her expertness in steaming through the meshes of the law."[82] De Lome was accused of spending $15,000 a month in detective work in trying to "head off filibusters."[83]

Filibustering activities were evidently exaggerated by newspapers, in some instances unintentionally. It was natural that the press should carry accounts of expeditions leaving the United States, but only occasionally was it able to report whether or not the vessels were successfully landed in Cuba. In consequence, Spanish authorities were given the impression that expeditions were sailing openly and that the authorities of the United States were doing little to prevent their departure, or to effect their capture, when such was not the case.

There was no subtlety in the means employed by sensational newspapers to build favorable sentiment for the Cubans. Reports of filibustering expeditions brought protests from Spanish authorities which in turn occasioned sharp criticism from the press. Some editors either gave little consideration to the merits of the various cases that arose or else purposely misrepresented facts. Therefore, filibustering activities from the beginning of the revolt furnished sensational journals with opportunities for keeping the insurrection before the American public and for making bitter attacks against Spanish policy.[84] The "Allianca" affair was the first of a series of filibustering controversies which stirred the indignation of the press throughout the country and again brought up the old question of the purchase or annexation of Cuba.[85] These expeditions also caused serious diplomatic entanglements between this country and Spain and obviously contributed materially toward bringing about strained relations between the two nations.

---

[79] *Journal*, Jan. 3, 1897, 1.
[80] *Ibid.*, Jan. 6, 1897, 1.
[81] *World*, Oct. 18, 1897, 7.
[82] New York *Sun*, June 9, 1897, 6.
[83] *Journal*, Dec. 2, 1897, 1.
[84] *Times-Herald*, March 16, 1895, 5.
[85] *Idem.*

CHAPTER III

SPANISH "ATROCITIES" IN CUBA

General Campos, head of the military forces of Cuba, was recalled by the Spanish government early in 1896 because of his inability to deal effectively with the revolt, and Valierono Weyler was named Captain-General. Weyler was not unknown to the American public. He had served Spain in previous revolts and had gained the reputation of being "the most brutal and heartless soldier to be found in a supposedly civilized country."[1]

Before Weyler arrived in Cuba, it was freely predicted by the press that he would "cause the island to flow with gore." He was referred to as the "modern imitator of Cortez," the slayer of defenseless women and children. This conviction on the part of the press was strengthened when a dispatch from Madrid announced that the new military leader would adopt a much more drastic policy in dealing with the revolt than his predecessor had pursued. In view of the fact that the press generally had been critical of the Spanish policy under Campos, the announcement of the new appointment might have been expected to cause general alarm in the camp of Cuban sympathizers. Spanish atrocities in Cuba during the year of 1895 had been dwarfed only by those of the Turk in Armenia, it was charged, but they were not "great enough to satisfy the thirst for blood inherent in the bull-fighting citizens of Spain." If the slaughter of women and children had not been on a large enough scale, one newspaper stated, the Cuban sympathizers in this country wondered to what greater extent the Spanish oppressors could carry their policy of butchery. But Spain was warned that if the outrages of the past were exceeded, the American people would "rise up and drive from their doors the last vestige of that race which has plundered and murdered its conquered from the time of Cortez and Pizarro to that of Campos."[2]

Captain-General Weyler lost no time in disclosing his "new policy." It was reported "unofficially" that he had

---

[1] Chicago *Times-Herald,* Jan. 20, 1896, 6.
[2] *Idem.*

issued a proclamation before he left Spain giving the rebels just ten days in which to lay down their arms, after which he proposed to adopt "severe measures."[3] If these "severe measures" meant a vigorous campaign against the Cubans in the field, which the partisan press seriously doubted, all would be well, but if Weyler proposed a policy of massacre or of war on non-combatants, which the press felt fairly certain he would adopt, Spain was forewarned that the American people "could not possibly maintain their neutrality."[4]

Weyler issued his famous order in February, 1896, requiring the people of Cuba to concentrate about military headquarters maintained over that area controlled by the Spaniards.[5] There was to be no traveling without passes, the commercial establishments of the island were to be at the disposal of the commanders, and the population was to be completely under the control of the military department.[6] Thus was Weyler's "Reconcentrado" program definitely begun.

The New York *World* said that this order virtually placed under arrest the population of entire districts and confiscated the property of their merchants at the pleasure of General Weyler's subordinates.[7] It also stated that this vigor against non-combatants was in keeping with the policy of that "long line of narrow-minded military dictators whose pusillanimous rigor in dealing with the defenseless cost Spain her colonies." Weyler proposed to convert the war into barbaric butchery, the Pulitzer paper asserted, denying to his opponents the rights that all civilized nations accord to "armed insurgents" everywhere:[8]

> We love liberty and hate despotism. Our minds revolt at such cruelties as the Spanish inflicted upon Cubans in the last war and now threaten to repeat.

With the partisan press assuming such an attitude regarding Weyler even before his program was well under way, it is not surprising that opposition increased as time passed.

By the time Weyler began his "Reconcentrado" program, four New York newspapers—the *World, Sun, Journal,* and

[3] *World,* Feb. 12, 1896, 6.
[4] *Times-Herald,* Feb. 12, 1896, 6.
[5] *World,* Feb. 17, 1896, 1.
[6] *Ibid.,* 6.
[7] *Ibid.,* Feb. 18, 1896, 6.
[8] *Ibid.,* March 2, 1896, 6.

Herald, had correspondents on the island. In addition, the Washington *Post* and the New Orleans *Times-Democrat,* and several Florida newspapers were maintaining reporters in Cuba. *World* and *Journal* "artists" accompanied their correspondents to make sketches for use in connection with the day's news. From this corps of newspapermen a continual stream of atrocity stories flowed, the nature of which grew more sensational as Weyler's policy began to cause suffering among the peasants huddled in the military camps. Weyler's plan was to bring the loyal people together so that all those found outside the camps might be summarily dealt with.[9] Both Spaniards and rebels now began a systematic campaign of destruction. Fields were laid waste, livestock driven off, and plantation houses and sugar mills were burned.[10] Soon, food in the military camps of the interior became scarce, and suffering was intense. The newspaper correspondents made the most of their opportunities. Pushing into the interior, if they were successful in evading Spanish patrols, the reporters wrote news articles dealing with atrocities and suffering among the Cubans, while "artists" sketched pictures intended to give visible proof of conditions, supposedly obtained from observation.[11] When correspondents were unable to go beyond Havana, news articles and pen sketches, depicting "actual" scenes in the "Reconcentrado" camps, continued to be sent out daily.[12] These dispatches, the press stated, were smuggled aboard vessels bound for Key West or other points along the Florida coast, whence they were transmitted by telegraph to the newspapers.

The most persistent of the New York newspapers in obtaining atrocity stories were Pulitzer's *World* and Hearst's *Journal.* Following the lead of these two papers, the partisan press continued the publication of atrocity stories throughout the period of Weyler's rule in Cuba, which lasted until the fall of 1897. As the leaks in Weyler's censorship became apparent to the Spaniards, there was a general tightening up of restrictions and finally, most of the correspondents were expelled from the island, after which they were obliged to pick up their stories as best they could.[13] Taking into account

[9] *Ibid.,* Feb. 18, 1896, 6.
[10] *Ibid.,* April 21, 1896, 1.
[11] Milwaukee *Sentinel,* April 18, 1898, 4.
[12] Boston *Herald,* July 28, 1896, 12.
[13] *Ibid.,* June 9, 1896, 6.

the difficulty encountered by the reporters, both in obtaining news and in sending it out, it is reasonable to assume that there were good grounds for the charges made by a group of newspaper editors that many of the correspondents wrote their atrocity stories at Key West where abundant Cuban propaganda could be obtained from the Junta.[14] That their news reports were inaccurate is evident.

When the *World* sent Creelman to Cuba early in 1896, he wrote such sensational news stories of the conditions of the Cubans in the "Reconcentrado" camps that he was ordered by Weyler to leave the island. But the correspondent, according to the *World,* remained in Havana and continued to send out each week several columns of news articles of alleged Spanish atrocities. Typical of the type of atrocity story he wrote is the following:[15]

> No man's life, no man's property is safe. American citizens are imprisoned or slain without cause. American property is destroyed on all sides. There is no pretense at protecting it. . . . Millions and millions of dollars worth of American sugar cane, buildings and machinery have already been lost. This year alone the war will strike $68,000,000 from the commerce of the U.S. . . . Wounded soldiers can be found begging in the streets of Havana. . . . Cuba will soon be a wilderness of blackened ruins. This year there is little to live upon. Next year there will be nothing. The horrors of a barbarous struggle for the extermination of the native population are witnessed in all parts of the country. Blood on the roadsides, blood in the fields, blood on the doorsteps, blood, blood, blood! The old, the young, the weak, the crippled—all are butchered without mercy. There is scarcely a hamlet that has not witnessed the dreadful work. Is there no nation wise enough, brave enough to aid this blood-smitten land? Is there any barbarism known to the mind of man that will justify the intervention of a civilized power? A new Armenia lies within 80 miles of the American coast. Not a word from Washington! Not a sign from the president!

[14] *Cf.* Chicago *Times-Herald,* Feb. 19, 1898, 6; New York *Evening Post,* March 28, 1898, 6; New Orleans *Times-Democrat,* Feb. 18, 1898, 6.

[15] *World,* May 17, 1896, 1.

Editorially, the *World* argued that the misery that threatened the unfortunate island could be averted only by the "kindly services" which might be tendered in accordance with a concurrent resolution then before Congress.[16]

Creelman continued to write articles likely to arouse sympathy for the Cubans as well as revulsion for Spanish atrocities.[17] As the resentment of the Spaniards against the correspondents came to be more openly expressed, the news stories seemed to embody more details of cruelties and suffering and torture.[18] News stories, dealing with many forms of Spanish "atrocities," were smuggled from within Havana to the *World*. Hospitals were invaded and inmates were lined up and shot, it was charged, while helpless women and children looked on. Men, women, and children, the newspaper asserted, were found dead in heaps by the roadside, the victims of famine and disease. Each news account was illustrated with pen sketches made by an "artist" from the impression obtained from the news report.

Another *World* news article, rivaling for sordid details the one written by Creelman, was the following:[19]

> The skulls of all were split to pieces down to the eyes. Some of these were gouged out. All the bodies had been stabbed by sword bayonets and hacked by sabres until I could not count the cuts; they were indistinguishable. The bodies had almost lost semblance of human form. The arms and legs of one had been dismembered and laced into a rude attempt at a Cuban five-pointed star, and were satirically placed on the breast of a limbless form. The tongue of one had been cut out, split open at the base and placed on the mangled forehead in a ghastly likeness of a horn. Fingers and toes were missing. All the bodies were further mutilated and again arranged in a manner so indescribably repulsive as to prevent description. Two of the mouths were split back to the angle of the jaw, so as to give an untellably ghostly grin to each mangled face. And the ears were all missing. These could not be found and I was forced to the conviction of

[16] *Ibid.*, April 28, 1896, 6.
[17] *Cf. ibid.*, May and June, 1896.
[18] *Ibid.*, May 29, 1896, 7.
[19] *Idem.*

> what I had often heard but never believed, that the Spanish soldiers habitually cut off the ears of the Cuban dead and retain them as trophies. Our Indians were more cleanly than this.

The account was written by Sylvester Scovel and the facts were supposedly obtained by him on a visit to Pinar del Rio. Scovel continued to write similar stories of conditions which he said were found in the provinces near Havana.[20] These news reports were from two to five columns in length ordinarily and were well illustrated with pen sketches. The *World* correspondents emphasized the alleged treatment by the Spanish soldiers of women and children. A good illustration of this type of news story is the following, apparently written by Scovel:[21]

> "I'll make you," said the Spaniard, and he proceeded to tear off her clothing. He then questioned her anew and receiving no answer from the woman who was crying hysterically he unsheathed his sword and fell to cutting and slashing his victim, until her blood covered the floor and she fainted in a corner. Her shrieks and entreaties only served to provoke the brutal laughter of the soldiery. . . . With a convulsive movement the woman tried to shield her child with her own body, but the merciless bullets did their work. . . . The baby was not killed outright and one of the soldiers, moved by a sort of barbarous pity, crushed the little one's skull with the butt of his rifle. . . . A score of machetes flashed and in a few moments the prisoners were a mass of blood and rags. A drunken fancy seized the murderers. Cutting off the heads of their victims, they hung them to the key of the grocer's door, while the horror-stricken neighbors looked on without daring to interfere. Only under cover of night were the ghastly remains removed and buried.

The article was obviously based upon the account of the incidents as related by a Cuban eye witness. It was well illustrated with sketches and "photographs made on the spot." Many of Scovel's articles were based upon accounts of sup-

[20] *Ibid.*, June 1, 1896, 1.
[21] *Ibid.*, June 8, 1896, 7.

posedly eye-witnesses to "atrocities."[22] Some of these accounts were furnished by Spanish soldiers "who spoke of massacres as if they were every day occurrences with them."

Despite the revolting stories it had been carrying daily, the *World* came out with the statement: "The Worst Has Not Been Told; Even Little Children Are Slain by the Spanish; Bodies Sometimes Shamefully Mutilated."[23] One news story told of how a "drunken Spanish major" had killed peaceable Cubans because they lacked enthusiasm and how the entire town was saved when a sober lieutenant "interrupted the slaughter by a call 'to horse.' "[24] According to the *World,* members of the Red Cross were not permitted to bury the dead, and the bodies were eaten by dogs. Officers who killed the most peasants were promoted and decorated, it was charged, and the children of Spanish families of high standing asked for Cuban ears for play things.[25] These articles were written by Scovel.

Occasionally the *World* carried news stories telling about atrocities perpetrated on Americans.[26] One of these stated that Spanish bands robbed and burned the homes of Americans in Cuba and killed their employes. The only offense charged against them, the *World* said, was the "unpardonable crime of being Americans." The newspaper stated also that outrages on Americans were committed at Sagua and that when protests were made by the American diplomatic agent he was scorned. Victims were mutilated, the Pulitzer paper contended, before being shot down in cold blood. These stories of outrages, the *World* asserted, could be verified easily by the government at Washington. In addition to Scovel and Creelman, Gay was sent to Cuba to aid in the writing of atrocity stories. After the arrest of Scovel by Weyler, Gay continued to send out news articles regularly until he, too, was expelled from the island.

In daily editorials dealing with Spanish atrocities, the *World* urged the President to intervene to put a stop to "the slaughter of innocent women and children."[27] The newspaper stated that "the camera does not lie" and that Spanish

---

[22] *Ibid.*, June 4, 1896, 1.
[23] *Ibid.*, June 5, 1896, 7.
[24] *Ibid.*, June 10, 1896, 1.
[25] *Ibid.*, June 20, 1896, 7.
[26] *Ibid.*, June 24, 1896, 7.
[27] *Ibid.*, June 1, 1896, 6.

atrocities had been confirmed by the camera.[28] And as if to lend greater credence to its atrocity stories, the Pulitzer paper pointed out that the date and places of the "murders and survivors' stories were investigated by the *World* correspondent."[29] Following this explanation was a long article telling how natives of Cuba were slain, their bodies thrown into trenches, and left unburied. Inoffensive men were tied up and shot, the Pulitzer paper stated, and one woman, who had fled in terror from the town, gave birth to a child on the porch of a grocery store. These stories were written by Creelman and were based on reports of "eye witnesses." In an editorial the following day, the *World* asserted that the Creelman article "bears on its face the evidences of its truthfulness" and that "it is wholly devoid of sensationalism or exaggeration."[30] The editorials repeated much of what had been included in Creelman's stories and sharply criticised the administration for not taking action to stop "the murders at our very doors." As if fearful that its atrocity stories were almost too sensational to be believed, the *World* reiterated that "the situation in Cuba has been laid before the American people with a fullness, clearness, and fairness which leave no room for doubt in the mind of any one" and that the "special correspondents of the *World* have reported the facts as they found them."[31]

The *World's* editorial comment varied from attacks on the administration to attacks on Weyler and his policy. Frequently, however, it devoted much space to discussion of conditions in the island. In one of its criticisms of Weyler, the *World* said:[32]

> If it were possible General Weyler would suppress all newspapers. He hates news. It interferes with his plans to see their execution faithfully reported in the newspapers even before he has had time to receive his official advices. Besides, it must disgust him to read in the press of the cries and groans of the wounded, of the splashing of blood, the heart-rending shrieks of the widows and orphans, and all the other incidents of

---

[28] *Ibid.*, June 25, 1896, 6.
[29] *Ibid.*, May 25, 1896, 1.
[30] *Ibid.*, May 26, 1896, 6.
[31] *Ibid.*, May 3, 1896, 6.
[32] *Ibid.*, May 8, 1896, 6.

> those fusillades by which Spanish authority maintains itself.
>
> It must not be supposed that General Weyler is a monster. He is merely a barbarian living in a civilized century. A few hundreds years ago our own ancestors chopped their fallen enemies out of their armor plate with axes and decapitated them if they could not pay ransom. A few centuries earlier, they used their skulls for drinking cups. But that was not monstrous or unnatural. It was merely barbaric and General Weyler is merely barbaric.

Weyler charged that Creelman was misrepresenting facts in Cuba and sent out a commission to investigate conditions in the camps.[33] Following its report, he issued an order banishing Creelman from the island. Creelman protested in an article to the Captain-General, a copy of which was displayed in the *World*. In this letter to Weyler, Creelman charged that his banishment was "a confession that you know the truth but shrink from having it known by the civilized world." Creelman contended that the evidence to which he had referred in his news articles "lie within eight miles of your palace doors." The correspondent concluded his communication by saying that his offense was that he had refused to print false news issued by the general staff of the Spanish army in Cuba, or to hide the blunders and defects of the Spanish forces in the field. Weyler later admitted, the *World* stated, that the charges made by it were true.[34]

The expulsion of Creelman did not affect the flow of atrocity stories for day after day the *World* carried columns of news telling of murders, multilations, and suffering.[35] One news article reported that 160 peaceable old men, young men, boys, and children were killed outright and in cold blood, of whom eighty-seven were "horribly mutilated," and that women were "shockingly abused and three girls were severely clubbed while striving to defend their honor."[36] In one edition, all of the front page except one column was devoted to Cuban news.[37] In this same edition, six columns

---

[33] *Ibid.*, May 14, 1896, 1.
[34] *Ibid.*, Sept. 18, 1896, 6.
[35] *Cf. ibid.*, August, September, October, and November, 1896.
[36] *Ibid.*, Sept. 18, 1896, 1.
[37] *Ibid.*, Nov. 30, 1896, 1.

were filled with a list of men and women alleged to have been killed by Spanish guerrillas, with the place given where the killings occurred, the age of each victim, the name of the Spanish force committing the atrocity, the number of dependents of each victim, and a brief account of the atrocity committed on each. According to this list, many mothers left from two to twelve children as dependents. The Pulitzer paper stated that the report was a "detailed, authentic list, with names and places of innocents slaughtered by Spanish guerrillas or regulars in Pinar del Rio Province" collected by a *World* correspondent and "supported by many affidavits of eye witnesses, now in possession of the *World*."[38] The newspaper asserted that soldiers were sent out disguised as farmers with orders to shoot all peasants in sight and prisoners were "butchered on the field and their mutilated bodies left for carrion." When male "pacificos" grew scarce, it was charged, the Spaniards attacked women and children. A few days later, the *World* said: [39]

> By the Captain-General's order the Cuban people, armed and unarmed, at war or at peace, have been given over to the bayonet and the machete.

In another atrocity story, the *World* asserted:[40]

> A great pit filled with corpses and human fragments was discovered Monday in a cane field not more than a mile from that place. A careful investigation revealed at least 20 whole bodies and many more legs and arms, other parts of the dismembered bodies being missing.
>
> Of the bodies remaining entire, four were those of women, three of young misses, one of a girl of not more than ten years old, four boys and the rest men.
>
> Permission to bury the bodies was brutally refused, with a threat that if this slaughter was complained of, many more would be added to what Spanish officials called the "Cuban dirt pile."
>
> No pen can fitly describe the awful scene of devastation and misery the island now presents. . . . A people is being butchered and a country destroyed.

[38] *Ibid.*, Sept. 18, 1896, 1.
[39] *Ibid.*, Sept. 21, 1896, 1.
[40] *Ibid.*, Jan. 8, 1897, 7.

The *World* quoted Gen. John M. Schofield as urging immediate intervention by the United States in Cuba to stop the conflict:[41]

> If you see any insane mother trying to murder her own child because it will not submit to torture, do you go home and consult your law books? No! You seize her by the throat if necessary, and save the life of the child.

Referring to the ravages of famine and disease in the island, the *World* stated that 200,000 people were starving to death, and that from sixty to seventy died daily from hunger.[42] Of the 200,000 "dying wretches" perhaps 3,000, the *World* added, were citizens of the United States engaged in peaceful pursuits. Several months later, the *World* said that "it appears now that nearly seventy-five per cent of the 400,000 helpless women, children and non-combatants affected by Weyler's savagery are dead."[43] Reporting that there were 1,500 dead on one plantation, the newspaper said that "the creek banks are absolutely filled with buried." Weyler's policy was referred to as being as cruel as that of Nero.

The number of Cubans who died as a result of the "Reconcentrado" system was undoubtedly large, but it is questionable whether or not the *World* correspondents, or any one else for that matter, were able even to approximate the figures for the reason that no record of deaths was kept by the Spanish military authorities. Even if such record had been kept it would have been unavailable to the correspondents. Estimates, based on the census report for the island before the revolt and that taken after the Spanish-American war, with allowances made for a normal increase in population, show that newspaper reports of deaths were highly exaggerated. The population of Cuba in 1894, the year before the revolt broke out, was given as 1,631,696.[44] The official census figures for 1899, one year after the Spanish-American war, were 1,572,845, showing a loss in population during the approximate period of the revolt and subsequent war of 58,851.[45] The population of Pinar del Rio Province,

---

[41] *Ibid.*, Jan. 29, 1897, 7.
[42] *Ibid.*, April 15, 1897, 1.
[43] *Ibid.*, Nov. 16, 1897, 1.
[44] *The Statesman's Yearbook, 1900* (London, 1900), 1196.
[45] *Report of the Census of Cuba, 1899* (Washington, 1900), 179.

where most of the deaths from starvation were reported to have occurred, in 1887 was 225,891; in 1899 it was 173,082, showing a loss during the twelve-year period of 52,809.[46] The increase in the island's population from 1861 to 1894 was only 235,166, or approximately 7,000 a year.[47] Allowing for an increase of 7,000 for the five year period, 1894-1899, the total would be 35,000, which may be regarded as the normal increase. This figure added to the 58,851 loss in population for the same period gives an estimated loss for the island of 93,851. This number is in striking contrast with that of "nearly" 300,000 reported by the *World* correspondent to have died of starvation.

During this period, the *World* carried many illustrations, most of them pen sketches with some photographic reproductions, intended to show the results of Weyler's policy and Spanish cruelties. One large illustration depicted a Cuban soldier with forty-two wounds on his body said to have been caused by Spanish machetes.[48] In another edition, a half page of pictures of starving Cubans was published with the caption: "World Photographs Taken Among the 200,000 Survivors of the 400,000 Cuban Non-Combatants Condemned to Death by Weyler's Order."[49] Cartoons dealing with the Cuban situation were used frequently, one of which showed "Famine" in the form of a hungry lion devouring an emaciated woman and child with the title, "And Spain Calls This War."[50] Another group of pictures of supposedly starving Cubans carried the striking caption, "Cubans Beg for American Crumbs."[51]

In what was one of its most effective editorials the *World* made a strong appeal to American sympathies for Cuban aid:[52]

> How long are the Spaniards to drench Cuba with the blood and tears of her people?
>
> How long is the peasantry of Spain to be drafted away to Cuba to die miserably in a hopeless war, that Spanish nobles and Spanish officers may get medals and honors?

[46] *Idem.*
[47] *Idem.*
[48] *World*, Nov. 18, 1896, 1.
[49] *Ibid.*, Nov. 14, 1897, 4.
[50] *Ibid.*, Nov. 9, 1897, 7.
[51] *Ibid.*, Nov. 19, 1897, 6.
[52] *Ibid.*, Feb. 13, 1897, 6.

> How long shall old men and women and children be murdered by the score, the innocent victims of Spanish rage against the patriot armies they can not conquer?
>
> How long shall Cuban women be the victims of Spanish outrages and lie sobbing and bruised in loathsome prisons?
>
> How long shall women passengers on vessels flying the American flag be unlawfully seized and stripped and searched by brutal, jeering Spanish officers, in violation of the laws of nations and of the honor of the United States?
>
> How long shall American citizens, arbitrarily arrested while on peaceful and legitimate errands, be immured in foul Spanish prisons without trial?
>
> How long shall the navy of the United States be used as the sea police of barbarous Spain?
>
> How long shall the United States sit idle and indifferent within sound and hearing of rapine and murder?
>
> How long?

In another editorial the *World* charged that the war in Cuba was the most brutal in modern civilized history,[53] and it urged the United States to insist either upon "civilized warfare in Cuba or upon the cessation of all war for the conquest of the island."[54]

That the *World's* atrocity stories were effective in drawing attention to Cuba is indicated by the direct references to these news articles made by speakers from time to time and by prominent persons quoted in interviews. Senator Chandler of New Hampshire wrote a letter to Cuban leaders in this country, which was read before a Cuban mass meeting held in Washington, in which he referred to newspaper reports of cruelties.[55] He advocated the sending of a "fleet to enter the harbors and an army to land upon the soil" of Cuba to put an end to the "atrocities." John Sherman, Secretary of State, was quoted as saying that the *World's* disclosures of horrors in Cuba were substantiated in the original report of Gen. Fitzhugh Lee, Consul-General at Havana.[56]

---

[53] *Ibid.*, May 15, 1897, 6.
[54] *Ibid.*, May 17, 1897, 6.
[55] *Ibid.*, May 17, 1897, 3.
[56] *Ibid.*, Nov. 8, 1897, 2.

The newspapers also stated that President McKinley expressed sympathy for the Cubans.[57]

De Lome was reported as saying that in case of war between the United States and Spain he did not know which would win, with reference to which statement the *World* said:[58]

> This remark of the Spanish minister made in seriousness by a diplomat of his standing is remarkable. It admits the tension in the relations of the two countries, and shows that the spirit of desperate bravado that would push Spain to war with the United States is not confined to the Spanish common people, but even affects those high in authority, who are better acquainted with this country's resources.

In discussing the possibility of war, the *World* published pictures of naval activities in the Brooklyn navy yard,[59] and intimated that the Atlantic squadron might be sent to Cuban waters.[60]

Senor Canavos, the Conservative Prime Minister of Spain, was assassinated in August, 1897, and Sagasta, a Liberal, came into power as head of the government, following which it was announced that Weyler would be removed and that General Blanco would be sent to Cuba as Captain-General with instructions to pursue a less severe course with respect to the treatment of non-combatants, though the "Reconcentrado" policy was not abolished until March, 1898.[61] With the dismissal of Weyler, the *World* abated its severe attacks against Spanish rule until the Maine disaster occurred.[62]

During the two years of 1896 and 1897, the *World's* circulation grew rapidly. At the beginning of 1895, its circulation was less than 400,000;[63] by April, 1896, the combined circulation of the *Morning World* and *Evening World* had reached 742,673 a day;[64] and early in 1898, it totaled 822,804.[65]

---

[57] *Ibid.*, Nov. 10, 1897, 1.
[58] *Ibid.*, Nov. 17, 1896, 7.
[59] *Ibid.*, Nov. 18, 1896, 2.
[60] *Ibid.*, June 23, 1896, 1.
[61] *Ibid.*, Nov. 12, 1897, 1.
[62] *Cf. ibid.*, October, November, and December, 1897.
[63] *Ibid.*, June 14, 1896, 6.
[64] *Ibid.*, May 1, 1896, 1.
[65] *Ibid.*, April 3, 1898, 6.

Hearst did not enter New York journalism until the fall of 1895, and it was not until 1896 that the *Journal* began a determined campaign for the Cuban rebels. The Hearst correspondents in Cuba matched the *World* reporters in the character and amount of striking news reports dispatched to this country, and by 1897 the *Journal* began to outdo the Pulitzer paper in obtaining sensational news. Richard Harding Davis, who was already a well known newspaper correspondent, and Frederic Remington, one of the most celebrated newspaper "artists" of the time, were sent by the *Journal* to Cuba in January, 1897, with a vessel at their disposal to convey news reports from Havana to Key West.[66] Soon, the *Journal* was receiving news stories of Spanish atrocities, well illustrated with pen sketches, that might have excited even the envy of Scovel and Creelman.[67]

Davis's first news article, a full page depicting the horrors of the Cuban revolt, appeared on January 31 with a whole page of illustrations sketched by Remington.[68] Davis, like the *World* correspondents, emphasized the alleged suffering and disease and famine found in the "Reconcentrado" camps. Like the *World* reporters, also, Davis seemed to have obtained most of his news from "eye witnesses" to atrocities attributed to Spanish officers and soldiers.[69] One of these accounts had to do with a "hero's story of torture in Cuba;" another dealt with an account of how the "Spaniards put a boy to death;"[70] still another bore the title, "Spanish Auction off Cuban Girls."[71] The Hearst paper was using the same type of appeal as that employed by the *World*.

Weyler had set up in the fall of 1896 what was known as the "Trocha," a cleared space about 150 to 200 yards wide made across the island through which was laid a military railroad.[72] Forts were built at intervals along this cleared space, beyond which was placed a maze of barbed wire. This barrier was established as a means of protection against any sudden attack from rebel bands. The *Journal* announced in February that Davis had viewed the "Trocha," having been the first correspondent to reach it.

---

[66] *Journal*, Jan. 17, 1897, 33. The drawings of Remington were familiar to thousands of readers of newspapers and magazines during this period.
[67] *Cf. ibid.*, February and March, 1897.
[68] *Ibid.*, Jan. 31, 1897, 3.
[69] *Ibid.*, Feb. 3, 1897, 1.
[70] *Ibid.*, Feb. 5, 1897, 8.
[71] *Ibid.*, Feb. 13, 1897, 2.
[72] *Ibid.*, Feb. 15, 1897, 1.

In other ways the *Journal* correspondents showed resourcefulness in getting news stories. Davis wrote a dispatch telling of alleged indignities practiced by Spanish officials aboard American vessels.[73] According to Davis's article, a "refined young woman was stripped and searched by brutal Spaniards while under our flag on the 'Olivette.'" Illustrations, based upon his impression of the incident as told in the dispatch, were sketched by Remington, one of which depicted a beautiful girl stripped to the skin by Spanish officers. The *Journal* evidently realized the possibilities of the story for it "played up" the report with a six-column headline with Remington's striking sketches. The effect of the dispatch was immediate. On the following day, the *Journal* carried in four-column type a reply from De Lome, displayed with the Minister's picture.[74] He was quoted as saying that Spain had a "perfect right to search an American vessel without the captain's consent." The newspaper also carried a dispatch from Washington announcing that Senator Cameron would introduce a resolution in Congress dealing with the matter of Spain's searching women on board American vessels. Hearst's paper quoted Senator Gallinger of New Hampshire, Representatives Southwick of New York, Southard of Ohio, and Stone of Pennsylvania as favoring action by the government to protect its people, and Senator Wilson of Washington proposed the annexation of Cuba.[75] The *World*, however, was so provoked by this latest "scoop" that it sought to show up the "fake," producing the girl in question, who emphatically denied that the incident related by Davis had occurred. The Pulitzer paper raised such a scandal over the "invention of a New York newspaper" that Davis was obliged to explain to the *Journal* that his dispatch had not stated that the girl was searched by male officers. As a fact, he contended, she was examined by a police matron in the privacy of a stateroom while officers patrolled the deck, and the idea of her having stood disrobed before male examiners was entirely the product of the *Journal's* and Remington's imagination.[76] The Cameron resolution was not introduced.

---

[73] *Ibid.*, Feb. 12, 1897, 1.
[74] *Ibid.*, Feb. 13, 1897, 1.
[75] *Ibid.*, 2.
[76] *Cf.* Walter Millis, *The Martial Spirit.* (Cambridge, 1931), 68.

Typical of the *Journal's* atrocity stories was the following account of the "mistreatment" of a woman:[77]

> The experiences of Senora Rodriguez and of Senorita Sigarroa, as related by these unfortunate women to the *Journal,* ought to make every American's blood boil with righteous indignation.
>
> Senora Rodriguez was arrested because her husband was an officer in the Cuban army, locked up in a felon's cell, held incommunicado for three weeks with four other refined women and a company of blaspheming and degraded criminals, taken to Nuevitas in a box car, and thence by steamer to Havana, where she was confined in the House of Refuge for abandoned women, in eleven cells altogether; and after enduring all kinds of insults and privations, was finally sent to Key West through the offices of Consul-General Lee.

Speeches of members of Congress favoring Cubans were published in the *Journal* with an occasional striking paragraph set off in bold-face type. A paragraph from one of these news reports is given below:[78]

> Senator Mason told in impassioned language the story of the shooting of boys, the ravishing of women, and the sale of young girls. He described the herding of famishing American citizens in the small towns and villages.

The *Journal* carried news articles written by members of Congress on the Cuban situation, one of which was contributed by Representative Money of Mississippi who told of how the Spaniards "attack hospitals, butchering the wounded."[79] Hearst sent a woman correspondent, Marion Kendrick, to Cuba in August, 1897, to write feature articles.[80] She proved to be a prolific writer, and her stories received generous display.[81] In addition to Miss Kendrick and Davis, the *Journal* sent to Cuba George Eugene Bryson, who aided Davis in the writing of atrocity stories, and later, Julian Hawthorne, well known war correspondent, whose articles de-

[77] *Journal,* March 2, 1897, 6.
[78] *Ibid.,* May 19, 1897, 3.
[79] *Ibid.,* Jan. 12, 1897, 2.
[80] *Ibid.,* Aug. 17, 1897, 1.
[81] *Cf. ibid.,* September, 1897.

picting the suffering in Cuba started early in 1898.[82] Hawthorne's accounts were given prominent display with one issue carrying two pages of pictures representing emaciated women and children of Cuba, which the *Journal* claimed were photographs but most of which were obviously pen sketches.[83] One illustration, showing carrion crows picking the body of a dead Cuban while starving children stood nearby, bore the caption, "Last of a Family of Seven Waiting for Death."[84] A paragraph from one of Hawthorne's articles follows:[85]

> A third of the population has died. Hundreds more are dying daily in Havana and its environs alone; dying with accompaniments of misery and suffering almost inconceivable, wholly undesirable. They fall dead in the streets; they die before your eyes as you stand in the wretched pens where they are huddled together; they die with an agony of body which is equalled only by the hopeless anguish and forlornness of their minds. Until lately, when an attempt to relieve some of them was made in America, they die unpitied and uncared for.

According to its own statement, the Hearst paper increased rapidly in circulation during this period. The *Evening Journal* was started Sept. 28, 1896, in connection with the *Morning Journal* which at this time claimed a circulation of 407,000, the largest of any other morning paper in the country.[86] In early November of the same year, the *Journal* stated that its combined circulation was 1,506,634, but this figure obviously included the circulation of the *Sunday Journal* which then probably exceeded 500,000.[87]

The influence of the New York newspapers in publishing atrocity stories apparently was felt throughout the country. The Boston *Herald*, in order to compete with the *Journal* and the *World*, both of which were rushing early editions to Boston, was obliged to give prominent display to news reports from Cuba.[88] The activity of the Chicago *Tribune* in behalf of the Cuban rebels evidently influenced the news policy

[82] *Ibid.*, Jan. 17, 1897, 34; *ibid.*, Feb. 14, 1898, 2.
[83] *Cf. ibid.*, March 14, 1898, 4-5.
[84] *Ibid.*, March 16, 1898, 3.
[85] Chicago *Tribune*, Feb. 9, 1898, 4.
[86] *Journal*, Sept. 28, 1896, 1.
[87] *Ibid.*, Nov. 8, 1896, 1.
[88] *Herald*, Jan. 25, 1898, 6.

of the Chicago *Times-Herald,* which, although it was far from being conservative in its display of Cuban "atrocities," made repeated attacks upon its rival because of the latter's "thirst for blood."[89] The *Times-Herald* also criticized the *Tribune* for getting out so many "extras."[90] The San Francisco *Examiner,* which was "playing up" alleged Cuban atrocities, was instrumental in causing the San Francisco *Chronicle* to try to keep pace;[91] and the Associated Press, which, during the early part of the revolt, was in competition with the United Press, was also sending out "thrilling accounts of the horrors attendant upon his (Weyler) 'Reconcentrado' system.'"[92]

It is not surprising then under the circumstances that newspapers everywhere gave generous space to news stories emanating from Cuba. The Chicago *Tribune,* using during this period the same news service as the *World* and after 1897, the Hearst syndicate service also carried the same type of atrocity stories as these two papers. As early as 1895, before Weyler was sent to Cuba as Captain-General, the *Tribune* published news stories telling of alleged Spanish cruelties.[93] In editorials used in connection with these articles the *Tribune,* urging American intervention in Cuba, asserted that "if this be a Christian nation, if this be a nation of men, it will put a stop at once to the carnival of slaughter that appears to be in awful progress there."[94] It referred to the "wholesale butchery of old and young women, children and even infants" following which "shocking indignities were offered to the unfortunate victims before and after death." In commenting editorially on the proclamation issued in 1895 by Costello, Prime Minister of Spain, concerning the treatment of Cubans, the *Tribune* said:[95]

> . . . Why do we wait longer? Can it be possible that the great and powerful government of the United States will sit quietly by and see this people fighting for liberty, which is as dear to them as to us, crushed out and butchered, banished and exterminated by the Spanish oppressor? Is it not time to say to Spain,

---

[89] *Cf. ibid.,* Jan. 20, 1896, 6; *ibid.,* March 15. 1898, 6.
[90] *Ibid.,* April 8, 1898, 6.
[91] *Chronicle,* Feb. 6, 1897, 9.
[92] *"M. E. S." His Book, op. cit.,* 159-160.
[93] *Tribune,* Sept. 7, 1895, 12.
[94] *Ibid.,* Sept. 5, 1895, 12.
[95] *Ibid.,* Sept. 24, 1895, 12.

> "Take your flag out of Cuba and give the people their liberty"?

But it was not until after Weyler's appointment that newspapers began a persistent publication of atrocity stories. Following the lead of the *World* and using many of the same stories, the *Tribune* columns daily were filled with articles and illustrations dealing with Spanish "atrocities." It also gave generous display to the speeches of members of Congress denouncing reported Spanish cruelties.[96] After the arrest by Weyler of the Rev. Dr. Diaz, a Baptist minister and naturalized American citizen, the *Tribune* stated:[97]

> This wanton arrest of Americans on trumped up or imaginary charges and the inflictions of prison torture have become intolerable and it is time to impress the fact on General Weyler.

The *Tribune* carried news articles written by Creelman, containing the same details of "butchery and murder and rapine" as were published by the *World*.[98] The newspaper recited stories of alleged Spanish massacres in the Philippines and compared these with reported cruelties in Cuba. The Spaniards were accused of reviving the methods of the Inquisition and using machines of torture brought over to Manila by Dominican priests 200 years ago:[99]

> It would be impossible to present more convincing testimony of the revolting blood-thirstiness of the Spaniards than given in this restoration of long-forgotten tortures. Instruments that fitted the brutal instincts of two centuries ago, that are alluded to now by civilized people only with terror and sinking trepidation, are welcomed by the Spanish today as desirable agents of tigerish hate. . . .
>
> These revolting details of unspeakable cruelty show how close is the Spaniard of today at heart to the Spaniard of two and one-half centuries ago.

Under the headline "They War on Women," the *Tribune* told of how Spanish troops "butchered 300 non-combatants,"

---

[96] *Ibid.*, April 5, 1896, 3.
[97] *Ibid.*, April 5, 1896, 6.
[98] *Ibid.*, May 2, 1896, 2.
[99] *Ibid.*, Nov. 29, 1896, 28.

and "drunken soldiers perpetrated nameless cruelties."[100] The newspaper, after criticizing Cleveland's proposed message to Congress, asserted that the Cuban rebels were not Spaniards but Americans and that "American leaders have been guillotined, American residents have been expatriated, American women and girls have been ravished and then shot, American homes have been pillaged and burned, American business interests have been destroyed."[101] Continuing, the *Tribune* asserted:

> Meanwhile a cowardly American president and a cold-blooded American secretary of state sit calmly by and declare there is not a state of war in that unfortunate island which has been harried and devastated by war nearly two years. It is not only war, but uncivilized, barbarous, bloody war. It must stop. If the present administration will not stop it the next administration will take the responsibility of stopping it and will thereby earn the plaudits of all humane, civilized, patriotic, liberty-loving Americans.

Early in 1898 the *Tribune,* which had already started using the Hearst syndicate service, carried Julian Hawthorne's articles.[102]

Upon the announcement of the appointment of Weyler as Captain-General, the *Times-Herald* predicted a reign of cruelty and this prediction was apparently fulfilled, judging by the news stories it carried of Spanish atrocities. In one of its issues, the *Times-Herald* carried the following news article:[103]

> Never in modern history has there been a more horrible or sickening spectacle than that which attended the public garroting of five Cubans. The unfortunates had been sentenced to death as "murderers, violators and incendiaries," but their punishment was far worse than their alleged crimes. Official bungling ushered them into eternity with tortures that could hardly have been surpassed in the days of the Spanish inquisition.

---

100 *Ibid.,* Nov. 30, 1896, 1.
101 *Ibid.,* Dec. 3, 1896, 6.
102 *Ibid.,* Feb. 9, 1898, 4.
103 *Times-Herald,* June 23, 1896, 1.

Quoting Gen. Fitzhugh Lee, the *Times-Herald* said that the Consul-General was horror-stricken at the condition of affairs in Cuba, and that the "barbarities practiced by the Spaniards have terribly shocked his soldier nature." After March, 1896, the *Times-Herald,* realizing the wide sympathy of Americans for the Cubans and fearing that the Democrats might profit by this sympathy, elect a majority to Congress in the presidential election in the fall, and agitate the free silver issue, grew more belligerent in its attitude toward the Spaniards.[104] It said that "between war (with Spain) and free silver" it preferred war.[105]

The New York *Sun* correspondent in Cuba sent out atrocity stories which were given prominent display in the *Sun* and those papers using the *Sun* news service.[106] The attitude of Dana's paper toward the Cubans was very well set forth in the following paragraph from an editorial:[107]

> It is to Spain's dishonor that an unsoldierly general who violates the customs of uncivilized warfare, a ruffian who kills non-combatants, a military bungler who has not won a battle, a bully who is detested by his own subordinates and a poltroon who seeks safety at Havana, is kept in office in Cuba.

The Washington *Post* was open in its criticism of Spanish policy,[108] and the San Francisco *Chronicle,* which was as partisan as the *Sun,* the news service of which it was using, repeatedly referred to the "cruelties of Weyler" and denounced his rule in Cuba..[109] Both the Charleston *News and Courier,*[110] and the Cincinnati *Commercial-Gazette* favored the Cuban cause and both carried atrocity stories.[111] The News Orleans *Times-Democrat,* as seen by its attitude in the "Allianca" and "Competitor" controversies, was also sympathetic toward the rebels and critical of Weyler's policy.[112]

That the agitation of the Cuban question was not confined to newspapers is shown by the fact that several of the

---

104 *Ibid.,* March 8, 1896, 6.
105 *Idem.*
106 *Cf. Sun,* June 7, 1897, 2.
107 *Ibid.,* May 12, 1896, 6.
108 Washington *Post,* May 12, 1896, 6.
109 *Chronicle,* May 18, 1896, 6.
110 *News and Courier,* March 3, 1896, 1.
111 *Commercial-Gazette,* March 11, 1896, 1.
112 *Times-Democrat,* May 13, 1896, 4.

leading periodicals from time to time carried articles dealing with the revolt written by well known writers. Among these was an article written for the *North American Review* by Mayo W. Hazeltine, literary editor of the New York *Sun*, in which the author presented a detailed explanation of the Spanish governmental system for Cuba, pointing out that the Cubans before the revolt had almost no participation in the work of national legislation.[113] Hazeltine also criticized Spain's economic policy in Cuba and stated that a large portion of the island's taxes was used to pay high-salaried officials. Another article, written by Clarence King, geologist and author, set forth the cruelties of Spanish rule during the 400 years she had occupied the island and advocated that the United States cast its lot with the Cuban cause.[114]

Leslie's Weekly, rivaling the *World* and *Journal* in the type of atrocity stories and the striking illustrations that it carried, conducted a vigorous campaign in behalf of the rebels. At this time, this weekly publication had a circulation of some 65,000 and was considered one of the most popular of the periodicals.[115] In one of its articles, the magazine said:[116]

> As it seems to us, Congress should at once give expression to the feeling of the country as to the savagery which the Spanish commander has introduced into his campaign, and if a dignified remonstrance in the name of humanity fails to produce any effect, then a stronger argument may properly be resorted to in acknowledgment of the belligerency of the insurgents. A people who have declared again and again their abhorrence of the brutality of the Turk in Armenia cannot afford to look with complacency on atrocities hardly less inhuman perpetrated at its very doors.

One complete issue of *Leslie's Weekly* in March, 1896 was devoted to the Cuban insurrection.[117] In a later issue it referred to Weyler's policy as "cruel and inhuman and goes far to justify the insistence that outside nations would be warranted, on the grounds of humanity, in intervening in the

[113] Mayo W. Hazeltine, "What Shall Be Done About Cuba?" in *North American Review*, CLXII, December, 1896, 406-413.
[114] Clarence King, "Shall Cuba Be Free?" in *The Forum*, XX, September, 1895, 50-65.
[115] *Leslie's Weekly*, LXXXII, March 5, 1896, 15.
[116] *Ibid.*, 16.
[117] *Cf. ibid.*, LXXXII, March, 1896.

struggle now in progress.''[118] The magazine again referred to Spanish ''oppression'' in these words:[119]

> Reports continue to reach us of the harsh and inhuman policy pursued by the Spaniards in their dealings with the insurgents in Cuba. In some cases these reports mention cruelties which would disgrace a savage people. While insurgents captured in battle are not always butchered, they are in nearly every instance subjected to brutalities of the most outrageous character.

An article written for *Leslie's Weekly* by J. Frank Clark, entitled ''The Cuban Insurrection—Cold-blooded Spanish Execution of Prisoners of War,'' dealt with the alleged cruel manner in which captured rebels were shot down.[120]

The newspapers favoring the Cuban cause gradually stopped publishing atrocity stories after the dismissal of Weyler, and it was not until the *Journal* brought to light several sensational matters that the papers again vigorously took up the Cuban question. For at least eighteen months the press of the country had been filled with stories of Spanish atrocities. When other problems regarding Spanish policy arose later, the American public was well acquainted with the Cuban insurrection.

In their campaign for Cuban freedom, the partisan press, particularly the New York newspapers, was resorting to one of the surest methods of striking a responsive chord among their readers—the attack of Spaniards on defenseless prisoners, their wanton disregard for the rights of non-combatants, and their abuse of the rights of American citizens. Sensational publications, by emphasis on topics most likely to find ready appeal, were developing a type of crowd-mind so necessary in effecting action for the Cuban rebels. If their purpose was to arouse opposition to Spanish rule in Cuba, the newspapers used good judgment in the practices employed. This was not the first instance in history, however, of the use of such means in stirring up public indignation, nor was it the last as evidenced by the vast amount of propaganda of a similar nature disseminated during the World War.

---

118 *Ibid.*, LXXXII, March 26, 1896, 15.
119 *Ibid.*, April 16, 1896, 23.
120 *Ibid.*, April 28, 1896, 21.

Reports of Spanish atrocities were evidently exaggerated, and in some instances the product of the reporters' imaginations. The American public, therefore, was being given striking accounts of cruelties for which, in many cases, there was no foundation of fact, and "jingo" senators and congressmen apparently chose to forego discussion of pertinent economic issues to engage in debate on a subject relatively unimportant but which offered excellent opportunities for oratorical display.

The influence of the sensational New York press was manifestly great, not only by reason of the widely distributed news service, but because of the example set other newspapers.

CHAPTER IV

POPULAR REACTION TO CUBAN "OPPRESSION"

The effects on the American people of newspaper reports of Cuban "oppression" is difficult to determine and can only be approximated. The influence of the press in stirring up opposition to Spain can best be arrived at through a study of the activities of the public and Congress in behalf of the Cubans as reported by the press. Such activities included the introduction of measures affecting Cuba and debates in Congress, the holding of mass meetings to aid the rebels, the raising of money, enlistments in the Cuban army, and petitions and memorials to legislative bodies asking for American intervention in the island. Assuming that the press was the main source of information about Cuba, these activities were evidently the direct or indirect result of newspaper propaganda.

The influence of the press on Congress is shown in the frequent references to newspaper accounts of atrocities made by certain members of the two houses in debates on resolutions concerning the Cuban insurrection.[1] Senator Mason of Illinois read a newspaper article telling of atrocities, and when Senator Hale of Maine complained of this practice, the Illinois Senator asserted that it was the only means of getting information concerning affairs in the island.[2] Senator Mason had been accused of reading from newspapers in previous debates.[3] Senator Turpie of Indiana, in arguing that the United States should take steps to end the conflict in Cuba, read excerpts from a newspaper,[4] and Senator Cannon of Utah read from the New York *Herald* and the Chicago *Tribune,* referring to the latter as "a paper which can not be charged with Cuban sympathies."[5] This statement sounds absurd in the face of the overwhelming evidence showing that the *Tribune* was only exceeded in its partisanship by the Hearst and Pulitzer papers, if by them. The *Herald* was also decidedly pro-Cuban.

---

[1] *Cf. Cong. Rec.,* 54 Congress, 2 Sess., XXIX, Pt. 2, 1157, Jan. 26, 1897; *ibid.,* 55 Congress, 2 Sess., XXXI, Pt. 2, 1574, 1578, Feb. 9, 1898; *ibid.,* 55 Congress, 2 Sess., XXXI, Pt. 2, 1874, 1875, Feb. 18, 1898.

[2] *Ibid.,* 55 Congress, 2 Sess., XXXI, Pt. 2, 1578, Feb. 9, 1898.

[3] *Idem.*

[4] *Ibid.,* 54 Congress, 2 Sess., XXIX, Pt. 2, 1157, Jan. 26, 1897.

[5] *Ibid.,* 55 Congress, 2 Sess., XXXI, Pt. 2, 1574, Feb. 9, 1898.

One of the best illustrations of the influence of New York newspapers on Congress is seen in the reading by Senator Mason of one of Julian Hawthorne's articles telling of "horrors" in Cuba.[6] The article, which had been written for the New York *Journal*, had appeared in the Chicago *Tribune*.[7] Senator Mason, after reading the news story, which filled nearly two newspaper columns, alluded to Hawthorne as being a highly responsible correspondent "well known to many of us personally and a man who has a national reputation."[8] In view of the fact that the *Tribune* was the strongest Republican organ in Illinois and one of the most partisan in the country, Senator Mason's praise for what he evidently considered its own correspondent is significant inasmuch as the Senator himself was a staunch Republican. Indirectly, the Illinois Senator was giving his stamp of approval to the Hearst news service.

Whether or not the practice of using newspaper accounts of Cuban "oppression" in congressional debates indicates the influence of the press on members of Congress, or merely that these members, realizing its potential power over their constituency, were utilizing it to strengthen their own position can not be ascertained. In any event, the apparent result was the same.

The practice of utilizing newspaper reports of Spanish atrocities in debates had another decided and far-reaching effect—that of making available to Washington representatives of newspapers in every section of the country, as well as the news gathering organizations, sensational accounts of the Cuban insurrection, which would not have become available to many of the papers in any other manner. Conservative publications, which refrained from exploitation of the revolt and severely denounced other papers in this respect, were inclined to use portions of the debates, despite the fact that much of the material for such debates had been taken from sensational newspapers, because the charges made by the press were given authority when they were repeated by members of Congress. Therefore, in addition to the practices employed by those newspapers which seemed to favor the Cuban cause, Cuban propaganda in this way was made avail-

[6] *Ibid.*, 55 Congress, 2 Sess., XXXI, Pt. 2, 1875, Feb. 18, 1898.

[7] *Tribune*, Feb. 9, 1898, 4. It should be remembered that the *Tribune* at this time was using the Hearst syndicate service.

[8] *Cong. Rec.*, 55 Congress, 2 Sess., XXXI, Pt. 2, 1875, Feb. 18, 1898.

able to that portion of the press that had consistently refused to permit its columns to be used for the cause of the rebels.

Soon after the outbreak of the Cuban insurrection, mass meetings were held in many of the larger cities to aid the cause of the rebels and as news reports of "oppression" increased, these gatherings were held more frequently.

That the Junta and Cuban League, which were organized by Cubans in this country early in the revolt to assist their countrymen, were instrumental in arousing sympathy for the rebels can not be questioned, but both of these groups were working directly through and in co-operation with the press, and their efforts would have been largely ineffective had it not been for partisan newspapers.

At one mass meeting held in Philadelphia $577 was collected for the Cubans and subscriptions to the amount of $3,000 were received.[9] A meeting of Cuban sympathizers was also held at Jacksonville, Florida, which was attended by a United States district attorney and a United States marshal, at which speeches, emphasizing the strength of the rebels and suggesting that Congress would soon take action with respect to Cuba, were made by Cuban sympathizers.[10]

Activities of Cuban leaders and sympathizers came to be so openly carried on that Pinkerton agents, it was reported, were employed by the Spanish government to watch the movements of the rebels so that the authorities of the United States might be informed of violations of the neutrality laws.[11]

Sympathy for the Cubans was declared by a group of South Chicago citizens at a meeting at which officers were elected and addresses delivered.[12] The purpose of the gathering essentially was to inform the representatives of that district in Congress of the sentiment of the people. It was agreed that a body of "stalwart men" would be ready at a "moment's notice" to form a regiment to help fight against the Spaniards. Shortly afterwards, two meetings were held in Chicago to give expression to the feeling of sympathy for Cuba; and resolutions to Congress and "the American people," reviewing the "suffering of the Cubans" and asking Congress to recognize Cuban belligerency, were adopted by

[9] New York *Times*, March 3, 1895, 5.
[10] *Ibid.*, April 6, 1895, 5.
[11] *Ibid.*, March 8, 1895, 5.
[12] *Ibid.*, Sept. 23, 1895, 5.

acclamation.[13] The resolutions also urged "our fellow citizens throughout this country to assemble in mass meetings, to diffuse information and thus arouse, or rather deepen, the sympathy of our whole people with the Cubans in their heroic attempt to cast off the yoke of oppression and to achieve that independence and freedom which are the great highways to happiness and prosperity." The press and pulpit were also urged "with voice and prayer to continue their help to the righteous cause of the men who are so bravely fighting for home and native land." Discussing these meetings, the Chicago *Tribune* said:[14]

> Whatever may be the feeling of the rest of the country in regard to the Cuban struggle for independence there can hereafter be no doubt that the citizens of Chicago are heartily in sympathy with the brave people who are struggling to free themselves from the yoke of Spain. Central Music Hall, commodious as it is, proved much too small to hold the mass meetings a few earnest men had arranged for them last night, and the hundreds who were unable to obtain admittance gathered in another room to join in voting stirring resolutions and to listen to the eloquence of chosen speakers.
>
> Chicago, represented by its mayor, by its Common Council, and by hundreds of its foremost citizens, has spoken—first of all the communities of the republic. Now let other cities follow the example and roll up to Washington a tide of public opinion that shall sweep the sluggish men in the seats of Congress toward liberty.

A resolution, extending sympathy to Cuban patriots, was adopted by the South Carolina constitutional convention;[15] and upon the petition of prominent business men of Key West, the city commissioners ordered the Cuban flag to be displayed over the City Hall with the Stars and Stripes for one day following which there was much "rejoicing of the people."[16] It was announced a few days later that Governor Mathews of Indiana would speak at the Atlanta Exposition

[13] Chicago *Tribune*, Oct. 10, 1895, 1.
[14] *Ibid.*, 6.
[15] *Ibid.*, Oct. 3, 1895, 6.
[16] Boston *Herald*, Oct. 5, 1895, 1.

on "Cuban Independence Day."[17] The announcement stated that the Governor would advocate recognition of Cuban belligerency, which, it was reported, would be followed by immediate annexation of the island to the United States.

With the headline "Cuba's Cry Is Heard," the Chicago *Tribune* announced that a meeting was held in Washington, D. C., to express sympathy for the Cubans, at which resolutions were unanimously adopted asking that belligerency rights be accorded the rebels.[18] Following a meeting held in Philadelphia for a similar purpose, the *Tribune* commented that "when the Quakers begin to grow belligerent it is a sign that the country is getting stirred up," adding that such gatherings could not fail to have an effect on Congress.[19]

Several large meetings, apparently sponsored by the Cuban League, were held in New York during the month of November, 1895, at one of which was present Mrs. Cespedes, wife of the Cuban President.[20] Mass meetings were also held at Atlanta;[21] Jacksonville, Florida; Columbus, Georgia;[22] and Frankfort, Kentucky.[23] In addition, more meetings were held in Chicago and Washington.[24] At Jersey City the County Democratic Committee adopted resolutions calling on the government to recognize the Cuban Republic.[25]

An organization known as the "American Friends of Cuba" was formed in New York in 1896 to aid the Cubans, and a systematic circulation of petitions to Congress, asking for American intervention in behalf of the rebels, was begun by the group.[26] Three weeks after its organization some 300,000 signatures to petitions had been reported.

The cruelties attributed to Weyler were discussed in the home and the schools as indicated by the raising of money for the rebels in the schoolroom and the action of Chicago boys in burning the Spanish general in effigy.[27] This fact is significant because it shows how effectively Cuban propaganda was being disseminated.

---

[17] New York *Times*, Oct. 14, 1895, 5.
[18] *Ibid.*, Nov. 1, 1895, 5.
[19] Chicago *Tribune*, Nov. 6, 1895, 6.
[20] *Cf.* New York *Times*, Nov. 9, 1895, 5; *ibid.*, Nov. 24, 1895, 5; *ibid.*, Nov. 27, 1895, 5; *ibid.*, Nov. 28, 1895, 5.
[21] Chicago *Tribune*, Dec. 19, 1895, 2.
[22] *World*, Dec. 16, 1896, 2.
[23] Chicago *Tribune*, Dec. 21, 1895, 2.
[24] *Ibid.*, Dec. 20, 1895, 2; Boston *Herald*, May 17, 1897, 1.
[25] New York *Times*, Sept. 21, 1895, 1.
[26] *World*, Dec. 14, 1896, 2.
[27] Chicago *Tribune*, Dec. 31, 1896, 4.

Col. Ethan Allen, President of the Cuban League, issued a circular in 1897, asking ministers throughout the land to shape their services on July 4 (which fell on Sunday) so as to influence public opinion favorably toward the struggle of the Cubans for independence.[28] Whether or not there was widespread response to this appeal was not reported by the newspapers.

The Chicago *Tribune* promoted a plan for getting Americans to subscribe money to help carry on the Cuban rebellion, which was taken up by newspapers elsewhere.[29] The funds thus collected were turned over to the Cuban Junta in New York. It was "rumored" that a part of this money was used to bribe congressmen and unsympathetic newspapers.[30]

From the time of the outbreak of the Cuban revolt, agents of the rebels sought enlistments in this country for the Cuban army.[31] As the rebellion progressed, newspaper reports of enlistments appeared frequently, the recruiting apparently growing with the increase of news stories of Spanish "oppression."[32] Reports from all sections of the country indicated that enlistments were going on, the Chicago *Tribune* announced, in violation of the neutrality laws of the country. It stated that "Boston is on fire for 'Cuba Libre,' " and that 106 men of Butte, Montana, had signed the roll for the Cubans. A company of young men enlisted in Arkansas City; two companies in Denver; several companies in Des Moines; a company of sixty men in Portsmouth, Ohio; a group of twelve men in Zanesville, Ohio; several men in Springfield, Illinois; and in twenty-four hours 800 were enlisted by the Cuban Junta in New York City.[33] In Pittsburgh, members of the national guard resigned to fight for Cuba and a Spanish flag was burned in Lexington, Kentucky. Shortly afterwards, the Junta announced that it had more recruits than it could handle, for the difficult problem was to transport the men to Cuba.[34] Much of the drilling of these recruits was carried on near Boston. This announcement of the Junta, however, did not tend to lessen recruiting as shown by the enlistments reported at the following points: Kansas City, more

[28] *Review of Reviews*, XVI, June, 1897, 6.
[29] *Tribune*, April 14, 1896, 2.
[30] New York *Evening Post*, March 26, 1898, 1.
[31] New York *Times*, March 3, 1895, 5.
[32] *Tribune*, Dec. 16, 1896, 1. It should be noted that the latter part of 1896 and the early part of 1897 were the periods during which Weyler's regime was at its height.
[33] *Idem.*
[34] *Ibid.*, Dec. 17, 1896, 1.

than 300 enlisted; Kokomo, Indiana, eighty men; Louisville, 252 men; Minneapolis, several trained nurses; Pittsburgh, several men including one West Point graduate; Sterling, Kansas, several men; Shamakin, Pennsylvania, seventy-five men; St. Louis, twenty men; Tomah, Wisconsin, militiamen offered services; Topeka, Kansas, thirty men; Columbus, Ohio, between 250 and 300 men from the national guard; Omaha, a group of men enlisted; and St. Paul, about twenty-five sharpshooters.[35] By the latter part of 1896, 1,000 men had been sent from St. Louis to the Atlantic seacoast. An ex-Confederate colonel enrolled 100 men at one point in the South, and it was announced that many cities and towns in the Middle West could easily raise from fifty to 100 men each.[36] Denver reported that it had 1,000 men ready to leave for the Florida coast, and St. Paul enlisted forty-one men.[37] Another report stated that twenty young men from Illinois embarked for New Orleans to join sixty others from various parts of the union to aid the Cubans.[38] Fifty-five Texas cowboys were already fighting for the Cubans, and a company of Texas rangers was ready to go to Cuba to be joined there by a company of 200 recruited in Butte, Montana.[39]

Col. James C. McComb of Delaware offered to equip a regiment and pay all expenses for its transportation to Cuba,[40] and the Governor of South Carolina volunteered to lead his militia in person against the Spaniards.[41]

The "American Volunteer Legion," which began organization in 1896, by the spring of 1897 had companies in more than twenty states and carried on its secret muster rolls men who were pledged to start toward Cuba on twenty-four hours' notice.[42] The companies were composed of picked men, who would be ready to embark in a week from the time the money for their transportation was forthcoming. The neutrality laws would be evaded, it was proposed, by having the men move as individuals without organizing on American soil.

---

[35] *Ibid.*, 2.
[36] *Ibid.*, Dec. 18, 1896, 2.
[37] *Ibid.*, Dec. 19, 1896, 2.
[38] *Ibid.*, Dec. 9, 1896, 2.
[39] *Ibid.*, Dec. 10, 1896, 2.
[40] *Ibid.*, Dec. 21, 1896, 2.
[41] New York *Evening Post*, March 17, 1898, 6.
[42] New York *Journal*, April 17, 1897, 10.

These reports of activities in behalf of the rebels show that a strong influence, manifestly the result of newspaper accounts of Cuban "oppression," was making itself felt on the American people. It is possible that these reports were exaggerated, yet the frequent publication of such activities probably lent impetus to the movement to aid the Cubans. The influence of the Cuban clubs, as has been pointed out, evidently played a part in causing such widespread activity in this country, but the work of these groups was confined largely to the coast cities. Without the aid of the press, which obviously worked hand in hand with these organizations, the efforts of the Junta and League would have proved ineffective in inflaming public opinion against the Spaniards.

CHAPTER V

NEWSPAPER CAMPAIGN FOR CUBAN BELLIGERENCY

The question of the recognition by the United States of the belligerency of the Cuban Republic furnished a topic for debate in Congress almost from the outbreak of the revolt in the island. Beginning with the convening of Congress in the fall of 1896 until early in 1898, many resolutions dealing with Cuba were introduced. Most of these measures requested the President to take such action as would result in the speedy recognition of the belligerency of the Cuban rebels; some sought to recognize the Republic of Cuba as a free and independent government; and a few requested the President to use the good offices of the government to effect a peaceful settlement of the rebellion in Cuba. A bill, declaring that a state of war existed between Spain and the United States, was introduced in the House in 1897, but no action was taken on it.[1] Some of the resolutions were ordered printed in the journals; others were referred to committees, and those bearing on the same subject usually were combined into single measures, which were reported to the two houses for action.

It was not until Feb. 28, 1896, that a concurrent resolution, recognizing that a state of war existed in Cuba, was approved by the Senate,[2] and on April 6, by the House of Representatives.[3] The resolution was only an expression of the sense of Congress, and President Cleveland ignored it.

The sensational press from the beginning of the rebellion had urged recognition of the belligerency of the rebels, though what benefits were to be derived from such recognition the newspapers were not clear in explaining. Recognition of belligerency would have meant that Spain could search United States merchant ships on the high seas for contraband of war, would have bound the United States to stricter neutrality, and would have relieved Spain from responsibility for international obligations in the territories under insurgent control. The Cubans would not have profited by a recogni-

---

[1] *Cong. Rec.*, 54 Congress, 2 Sess., XXIX, Pt. 3, 2289, Feb. 25, 1897.
[2] *Ibid.*, 54 Congress, 1 Sess., XXVIII, Pt. 3, 2256, Feb. 28, 1896.
[3] *Ibid.*, 2629, April 6, 1896.

tion of their belligerency.[4] Without belligerency the rebels could purchase arms and munitions of war; they and their friends could go and come unharmed and unorganized to take part in the conflict; and they could sell their securities to those who would buy them.[5] More than this they could not have done had their belligerency been recognized, unless they had possessed a navy. Even had belligerency been granted, the Cubans could not have employed persons in this country to serve in their forces, nor have fitted out and armed vessels in American ports. On the other hand, under the rights accorded by belligerency Spain would have been invested by international law, as well as by the Treaty of 1795, with the international rights of belligerency, which she had not claimed, including the right of visitation and search on the high seas, and the capture and condemnation of American vessels for violation of neutrality. Recognition of belligerency would have enabled Spain practically to have ended the transportation of munitions of war for the rebels.[6]

It would seem then that recognition of belligerency actually would have aided Spain. It was the issue of the right of search and seizure on the high seas that had caused so much controversy in the cases of the "Allianca" and the "Competitor." The rebels had no navy to profit by the privileges accorded under belligerency, and it is questionable whether or not belligerency would have created any appreciable demand for Cuban bonds issued by the "de facto" government.

President Cleveland steadfastly refused to agree to recognition of belligerency because he felt it to be impractical.[7] The newspapers seemed to assume, however, that recognition of belligerency by the United States would be a definite move in the direction of the independence of the island, and when President Cleveland declined to be influenced by the action of Congress, much sharp criticism was directed against him by the press.

The introduction of each resolution dealing with Cuban belligerency was the occasion for much debate in both houses of Congress, which was fully reported and commented upon

[4] *Cf.* John Bassett Moore, "Cuban Belligerency" in *The Forum*, XXI, May, 1896, 288-295.

[5] *Idem.*

[6] *Idem.*

[7] Richardson, *op. cit.*, IX, 719.

by a group of newspapers.[8] Senators and representatives, seemingly moved by the atrocity stories found in the press, made stirring speeches in favor of Cuban belligerency, using portions of the news reports from Cuba, and several newspapers reported these, repeating much of what they had previously used.[9] In this way the public was given a double portion of Spanish atrocity stories. The number of resolutions introduced in Congress dealing with Cuba and the speeches resulting from the introduction of such measures increased with the number of atrocity stories carried by the press.[10]

The newspapers that were active in obtaining atrocity stories were most critical of President Cleveland for his failure to take action toward aiding the rebels. One of the most outspoken newspapers in favor of the Cuban cause was the Chicago *Tribune*. As early as September, 1895, it started a campaign for belligerency rights for the Cubans which it continued until events began to move in the direction of war with Spain. Not only did the *Tribune* urge recognition of belligerency, but it frequently advocated the sending of battleships to Havana "to sink every Spanish vessel on the coast."[11] The *Tribune* contended that the Cubans had satisfied all the conditions necessary to securing recognition of belligerent rights,[12] and that "victory (for the rebels) is in sight if Uncle Sam will say the word."[13] Using the argument that Spain had waited only forty days before recognizing the Southern Confederacy during the War Between the States, the *Tribune* said that the rebels had been in the field over eight months and had defied successfully Spain's attempt by land and sea.[14] The newspaper asserted that when "Congress meets it should without delay notify Spain that the barbarous war she is carrying on in Cuba has lasted long enough."[15]

The *Tribune* conducted a poll of members of Congress to ascertain their attitude on the Cuban question and then with

---

[8] *Cf.* Chicago *Tribune*, New York *World*, New York *Journal*, New York *Sun*, New York *Herald*, Boston *Herald*, and San Francisco *Chronicle*, December, 1896, January and February, 1897.

[9] *Cf. World, Journal*, Chicago *Tribune*, and *Chronicle*, December, 1896, January and February, 1897.

[10] It was during the latter half of 1896 and the first half of 1897 that the press carried so many atrocity stories. During this same period some 25 resolutions dealing with Cuba were introduced in Congress.

[11] *Tribune*, Sept. 14, 1895, 12.

[12] *Ibid.*, Oct. 5, 1895, 12.

[13] *Ibid.*, Oct. 14, 1895, 1.

[14] *Ibid.*, Oct. 26, 1895, 12.

[15] *Ibid.*, Nov. 12, 1895, 6.

prominent display gave the results.[16] It also polled the governors of states regarding the Cuban situation, following which it announced that "with hardly an exception the governors believe that the government of the United States should not stand idly by to see a gallant people overthrown and the few liberties remaining to them utterly annihilated by one of the most tyrannical nations on earth."[17] It added that a consensus of opinion showed that the people of the United States were ready to aid the Cubans. Replies from only eleven governors were printed, however, which, in consideration of the total number queried, could not be regarded as showing conclusively the sense of the people of the United States.[18] This practice of polling public officials was used widely, not only by the *Tribune* but by the *World* and *Journal,* for the next two years. The *Tribune* also made an effective use of cartoons in its campaign for belligerency rights for the Cubans.[19] In addition to urging that belligerency rights be accorded the rebels, the Chicago paper strongly advocated recognition of the independence of Cuba as the only logical and practical solution of the Cuban question.[20]

After reporting that a Spanish editor proposed to lead 12,000 men in an attack against the United States, the *Tribune* announced that "Spain is hot for a fight."[21] Spain's alleged intentions toward this country were referred to in the following words:[22]

> Spain seems intent upon war with the United States. At least Spanish officials pretend to think war cannot be avoided. . . . The last utterances of Senor Canavos show that the chief preoccupation of the government is not war with Cuba alone, but the coming conflict with the United States.
>
> Few people in Madrid seem to doubt that this conflict will come if the Cuban war is not practically ended by the time McKinley or Bryan begins to govern.

Following the introduction in March, 1896, of a resolution in Congress recognizing the belligerency of Cuba, students

---

[16] *Ibid.*, Sept. 21, 1895, 1.
[17] *Ibid.*, Sept. 30, 1895, 3.
[18] *World*, Oct. 1, 1895, 1.
[19] *Tribune*, Sept. 21, 1895, 1; *ibid.*, Jan. 24, 1896, 1.
[20] *Ibid.*, March 15, 1896, 34; *ibid.*, Dec. 4, 1896, 4.
[21] *Ibid.*, April 3, 1896, 2.
[22] *Ibid.*, Aug. 15, 1896, 1.

in Spain stoned the American Consulate at Barcelona.[23] This action was interpreted by the *Tribune* as meaning that Spain was eager for war.[24] Referring to this incident, it said that "if Spain insists on fighting the United States the feeling here is that it can be accommodated."[25]

The news from Spain dealing with reported uprisings, the feeling of the Spanish people toward the United States, and Spain's alleged preparations for war with this country came from the *World's* special Madrid correspondent, Arthur E. Houghton, whose news dispatches were included in the regular service furnished other papers.[26] Madrid proved to be almost as good a source for news as Cuba, and the *Tribune,* as well as the *World,* gave Houghton's articles prominent display. The New York *Journal* also maintained a correspondent in Madrid.

The *Tribune,* in urging Congress to pass a measure providing $10,000,000 for national defense, advocated the spending of "millions to make the United States the equal if not the peer of any nation on earth," adding that "if millions will not do, let us take billions."[27] The Medill paper, insisting that strong defense measures be taken, estimated that the United States could raise an army of 9,467,694 men.[28]

The discussion of the danger of war with Spain was continued by the *Tribune* for several weeks. While the navy was being placed on a war footing, in anticipation of possible trouble with Spain, the army was equally active in its warlike preparations, the newspaper stated, especially along the South Atlantic coast.[29] After discussing at length the reported plans for war being made by the Navy Department, it remarked:[30]

> The United States would have no difficulty in whipping Spain if that country should presume to test our strength. We have better ships and more of them than Spain, and it would not be long after the beginning of such a war that the Cubans would possess

23 *Ibid.,* March 2, 1896, 1.
24 *Idem.*
25 *Idem.*
26 *Ibid.,* Aug. 15, 1896, 1.
27 *Ibid.,* March 2, 1896, 6.
28 *Ibid.,* March 10, 1896, 6; *ibid.,* March 12, 1896, 6.
29 *Ibid.,* Nov. 13, 1896, 1.
30 *Ibid.,* Nov. 14, 1896, 12.

> the entire island and the Spanish army would be imploring for transportation home.
>
> It would be vastly more honorable in the United States to set its navy to humbling Spain than to continue the present work of acting the spy and policeman for that country. Its mission seems now to be only to capture petty consignments of supplies and ammunition sent by Cuban sympathizers in this country to the fighting patriots.

The *Tribune* contended that the independence of Cuba "must be recognized and if Spain wants to go to war about it the war will be a welcome one, and she will get all the fighting she wants."[31] Basing its news article on the reports of passengers arriving in this country from Cuba, the newspaper asserted that "Spanish forces are talking of attacking this country."[32] The day before President Cleveland was scheduled to deliver his message to Congress, the *Tribune* announced that the proposed message "is interpreted as warlike" and that "it means a crisis for Cuba."[33] As a fact, the President's message was anything except "warlike." He suggested that Spain grant home rule to Cuba, but he did not favor the granting of belligerency rights to the rebels for the reason that they were not maintaining the status of a belligerent group.[34] After the message had been delivered, the *Tribune* admitted that it was disappointed and referred to the communication as a "makeshift and a time-server."[35]

One of the fallacious arguments used by the *Tribune*, and by other newspapers, in urging recognition of belligerency was that such action would permit the legal sale of arms and ammunition to the rebels.[36] The people of this country had such a right without belligerency, and no question was raised either by the government of the United States or Spain regarding the infringement of such a right. What the *Tribune* and *World*, either purposely or in ignorance, confused with the right of private citizens to sell arms to the Cubans was

---

[31] *Ibid.*, Nov. 28, 1896, 12.
[32] *Ibid.*, Dec. 16, 1896, 1.
[33] *Ibid.*, Dec. 8, 1896, 1.
[34] Richardson, *op. cit.*, IX, 719.
[35] *Tribune*, Dec. 8, 1896, 6.
[36] *Ibid.*, Nov. 2, 1895, 12.

the objection to the fitting out of filibustering expeditions from the United States.

With the convening of the second session of the fifty-fourth Congress, a controversial question arose that resulted in wide discussion, both in Congress and in the press. This was concerned with the right of Congress to pass a joint resolution recognizing the independence of Cuba over a presidential veto. A resolution recognizing Cuban independence, introduced by Senators Cameron of Pennsylvania and Call of Florida early after the convening of Congress in December,[37] was amended slightly in committee and given a favorable report.[38] In its amended form, the measure provided, in addition to recognition of independence, that the United States "will use its friendly offices with the government of Spain to bring to a close the war between Spain and Cuba."[39] The substitution by the committee of the word "will" for the word "should" made the resolution much stronger, and it was freely predicted that in the event the measure became effective it would result in intervention in Cuba and war with Spain.[40] Cuban sympathizers in the Senate began to talk of passing the resolution over the President's veto should it be disapproved. Meanwhile, Secretary of State Olney announced that Cleveland would not recognize the independence of the island even though Congress were to pass the resolution over his veto.[41] Secretary Olney explained that recognition was an executive power which could not be usurped by Congress. His contention aroused much opposition, and several newspapers sought the opinions of members of Congress through polls and interviews.[42] The opponents of Secretary Olney's opinion held that Congress derived its powers in regard to international relations from that part of the constitution giving Congress the right to regulate commerce with foreign nations, to define and to punish piracies and felonies committed on the high seas and offenses against the law of nations, to declare war, and to grant letters of marque and reprisals. The President on the other hand, it was correctly asserted, is empowered by

[37] *Cong. Rec.*, 54 Congress, 2 Sess., XXIX, Pt. 1, 39, Dec. 9, 1896.
[38] *Tribune*, Dec. 20, 1896, 2.
[39] Boston *Herald*, Dec. 19, 1896, 1.
[40] *Ibid.*, Dec. 20, 1896, 6.
[41] *Ibid.*, 1.
[42] *Ibid.*, Dec. 19, 1896, 9; New York *Journal*, Dec. 18, 1896, 1; New York *World*, Dec. 19, 1896, 1; Chicago *Tribune*, Dec. 20, 1896, 1.

the constitution to "receive ambassadors and other public ministers." It was this provision in the constitution, it was stated, which gave him exclusive jurisdiction in the recognition of other nations. Cuban partisans referred to the case of Texas, the independence of which, they insisted, Congress had recognized by separate joint resolutions. President Andrew Jackson gave his approval to the course taken in the Texas case, it was argued, because Congress had sole authority to declare war and to make appropriations for carrying on war and might well take the initiative in action which might lead to war.

The parties to the controversy received little enlightenment from an examination of the constitution both in the matter of executive powers versus legislative powers and the right to pass resolutions over presidential vetoes. Regarding the latter, the constitution says:[43]

> Every order, resolution, or veto, to which the concurrence of the Senate and House of Representatives may be necessary (except on a question of adjournment) shall be presented to the president of the United States; and before the same shall take effect, shall be approved by him, or, being disapproved by him shall be repassed by two-thirds of the Senate and the House of Representatives, according to the rules and limitations prescribed in the case of a bill.

Although the requirement of the constitution seems specific, the practice of Congress has been to present to the president for approval only such resolutions as are legislative in effect.[44] In brief, the nature and substance of the resolution, and not its form, controls the question of its disposition.

The *Tribune* asserted that Secretary Olney was defying Congress, and that members were "furious" over the announcement of his view denying the legality of a resolution passed over a presidential veto.[45] The newspaper went so far as to imply that "if the President endorses the Secretary's position and refuses to obey a law of Congress passed over his veto he would be impeached." Several other newspapers concurred in this view. The *Tribune* said that this

[43] Ascher C. Hinds, *Precedents of the House of Representatives* (Washington, 1899), IV, Sec. 3482, 329.
[44] *Ibid.*, IV, Sec. 3483, 329.
[45] *Tribune*, Dec. 20, 1896, 1.

country was "on the brink of war" with Spain as the result of the approval of the resolution by the Senate Committee on Foreign Relations.[46]

The opposition of Secretary Olney apparently killed the resolution.[47] The Boston *Herald* said that his action was "to nip a war scare in the bud" and that there was no longer "any danger of serious mischief therefrom." The *Tribune,* however, was not content to let the matter die so peacefully, and for several days it continued to agitate the "danger of war."[48] Obviously the controversy in this country over the Cameron resolution aroused the radical press of Spain, and the *Tribune* carried special dispatches from Madrid under such headlines as, "Canavos Talks of War," and "Spaniards Cry for War."[49] Holding out the promise for more decisive action with regard to Cuba when McKinley was inaugurated, the *Tribune* stated that the Republican party "was pledged to the cause of Cuba" and indicated that it would rest with that party "to aid suffering humanity."[50]

The Chicago *Times-Herald,* the *Tribune's* principal competitor, favored action by the United States looking toward Cuban aid, but it was much less vigorous in both news and editorial policy in this respect than the *Tribune.* Following approval by the Senate in 1896 of a resolution recognizing Cuban belligerency, the *Times-Herald* said:[51]

> We may expect the Madrid and Havana papers to yelp. But the resolutions will meet the enthusiastic approval of the American public, and if, incidentally, they convince the Spanish government that we are not indifferent to the aspirations of Cuba and do not regard this protracted war as of no importance to our own national interests so much the better.

Again discussing the question of belligerency rights, the *Times-Herald* stated:[52]

> The United States have a direct and material interest in the destiny and prosperity of the island. Far above this interest is the interest of humanity. It is

[46] *Ibid.,* Dec. 19, 1896, 1.
[47] *Herald,* Dec. 20, 1896, 12.
[48] *Tribune,* Dec. 20, 1896, 3.
[49] *Ibid.,* Dec. 28, 1896, 4.
[50] *Ibid.,* Dec. 22, 1896, 6.
[51] *Times-Herald,* Feb. 28, 1896, 6.
[52] *Ibid.,* March 4, 1896, 6.

> intolerable to the public sentiment of the United States that slaughter and pillage, due to political oppression, shall go on indefinitely at our very doors. The struggle Cuba is making for civil and political liberty is identical with the struggle the founders of the republic of the United States made against the selfishness and oppression of the crown of Great Britain. Thanks to the friendly aid of France, that struggle was brought the more speedily to an end. The struggle in Cuba ought to be brought to an end by the friendly aid of the United States.
>
> The American people do not want war with Spain. They do want an end of the era of blood, destruction and anarchy in Cuba. The voice of the Congress of the United States is patent, but not yet conclusive. . . .
>
> If Spain will not listen to friendly interposition for Cuba, the American people will not hesitate in due time to consider their responsibility as to Cuban independence or annexation of the island to the United States.

The New York *World* was quite as zealous in its efforts in behalf of Cuban belligerency as it was in uncovering alleged Spanish atrocities. In many respects its arguments were more logical than those of the Chicago *Tribune*. When a Madrid dispatch announced that the Spanish army already in Cuba was to be reinforced by six batteries and 30,000 men during the months of August and September, 1895, the Pulitzer paper effectively pointed out that "such facts as this leave no question of the belligerency of Cuba."[53] Like the *Tribune*, the *World* conducted polls of members of Congress as to their position with respect to the granting of belligerency to the rebels and published the favorable replies.[54] In one of these polls, three questions were asked: "What should be this country's attitude toward the Cuban insurgents? Should the United States recognize their belligerency? And should the United States annex Cuba?"[55] The replies were displayed in the *World* and were regarded by it as further evidence of the sentiment of the American people.[56] In referring to the sentiment of Americans for the Cubans, the

[53] *World*, July 21, 1895, 6.
[54] *Ibid.*, Sept. 21, 1895, 2; *ibid.*, Nov. 28, 1897, 3.
[55] *Ibid.*, Nov. 28, 1897, 2.
[56] *Ibid.*, Sept. 28, 1895, 1.

newspaper said that "if the press can be relied upon as an exponent of popular feeling the sympathy for the insurgents is on the increase in the United States."[57]

The *World* pointed out that one objection in the United States to the granting of belligerent rights to the Cubans was the fact that "much American capital is invested in Cuba."[58] With Spain contending that the Cuban affair was not a war but merely a domestic riot, Pulitzer's paper explained, Americans whose property suffered could demand indemnity "and get it if they are as lucky as Moro."[59] Should the United States declare that there was a war on the island, the *World* continued, "those Americans would stand a poor chance of getting compensation for damages."

In voicing his objections to the granting of belligerent rights, De Lome was quoted by the *World* as saying:[60]

> The rebellion in Cuba never would have been a serious matter at all had it not been for the interference of the United States. It never would have passed the limits of a mere riot had it not been for the money, supplies, arms and men that were sent from this country. Men have gone from this country with the assurances that the United States would extend belligerent rights to the Cubans and would in all probability send a fleet to Cuban waters to support the insurgents.

It was further charged by Duque Tetuan, Spanish Minister of Foreign Affairs, that the resolutions which Congress had adopted in 1896 in respect to the Cuban insurrection "are based on canards spread broadcast throughout the United States for the sole purpose of inflaming the passions of the people against Spain and awakening an unmerited sympathy with the insurrectionists."[61]

The *World* used cartoons in connection with its arguments for belligerent rights for the Cubans, one of which showed Cleveland as a bull in a ring prodded by the "Senate," the "House" and the "Press" and facing "Spain," the mat-

---

[57] *Ibid.*, Sept. 28, 1895, 6.

[58] *Ibid.*, Jan. 6, 1896, 7. It had been variously estimated that American investments in Cuba totaled some $50,000,000 (*Cf.* Chicago *Tribune*, March 4, 1896, 6).

[59] Moro was a naturalized American who had received large indemnity from the Spanish government for the destruction of a sugar cane plantation in the island during the "Ten Years' War."

[60] *Ibid.*, March 3, 1896, 1.

[61] *Ibid.*, March 5, 1896, 1.

ador, with the question "Will He Fight?"[62] Charging that Cleveland was trying to befog the Cuban issue before the people by "technicalities and international law and diplomatic usage," the newspaper predicted dire consequences for the administration should it "continue to ignore the will of the people."[63]

The *World* also deplored the "lack of defense in case of war" and urged Congress to take action to strengthen the American coast defenses.[64] It ran a six-column picture of the Spanish fleet with the caption, "Spain's Fleet Awaiting Orders to Lick Uncle Sam."[65] and later it compared the navy of the United States with that of Spain with the final comment that "Uncle Sam's chances for conquering amount to a certainty."[66]

In urging immediate action by Congress on the Cuban question, the *World* used the argument that Americans were being held in Cuban prisons without being accorded trials, that Cuban vessels attempting to trade with the United States had been fired on, and that "in one way or another we are giving Spain every advantage in the desperate and brutal struggle it is now making to prevent the further extension of our own fundamental principle of self-government which we have declared to be the inalienable right of all men."[67] It argued that "Weyler is being upheld by our action in preventing the Cubans from buying the arms, ammunition, medicine, clothing and other supplies which they have as much moral right to buy as Spain has." As has been explained, the government of the United States placed no restriction on the sale of arms to the Cubans.[68] In this respect also, the Pulitzer paper was misrepresenting facts to the American public.

The New York *Journal* was even more favorable toward the Cuban cause than either the *Tribune* or the *World.* By means of striking display of news stories, editorials and cartoons, it kept the Cuban question before the public, arguing consistently for recognition of the independence of the island and the intervention of the United States, if such were neces-

---

62 *Ibid.*, March 8, 1896, 1.
63 *Ibid.*, March 11, 1896, 6.
64 *Ibid.*, March 6, 1896, 6.
65 *Ibid.*, April 8, 1896, 5.
66 *Ibid.*, April 10, 1896, 5.
67 *Ibid.*, Nov. 19, 1896, 6.
68 *Supra*, 62.

sary, to stop the "Spanish slaughter." War with Spain would clearly have been welcomed by the *Journal*:[69]

> If we are going to give Spain what she chooses to consider a casus belli, the time to do it is now. She is steadily preparing for such a crisis. Her purchases of ironclads are manifestly directed against the U.S. She does not need them for the insurgents, who have neither navy nor fortifications. As yet we have a decisive naval superiority over her, but we are building our own ships, and it takes longer to build them than to buy them. If we intend to intervene for the liberation of Cuba, as a blind man can see we do, not later than next March, and probably not later than December, our obvious policy is to say to Spain, without another day's delay: "This anarchy in Cuba must stop —What do you propose to do about it?"

The *Journal* deplored the "scattering of the navy," which it asserted was not near enough to Cuba.[70] A few weeks later, it stated that the navy was ready for a war with Spain, and in connection with the news article pictures were used showing men at work on ten warships.[71] Asserting that the American people would be glad for a chance to join the rebels, the newspaper said that only a blow was needed to precipitate a conflict and that "Spain is capable of the folly of delivering it."[72] This prediction of the *Journal* was later fulfilled in the explosion of the Maine, which this paper attributed to Spanish treachery.

Weyler's defeat would mean war with Spain, the *Journal* contended, explaining that Spain would blame the United States for Cuba's loss and force hostilities.[73] It reported that dispatches from the navy yards showed that preparations for defense were being made everywhere, and that "from Maine to the Gulf work on vessels and fortifications is being pushed forward as rapidly as possible." The newspaper spoke again of the coast defenses and quoted General Miles as saying "be ready."[74] Charging that Spain was buying war material from Italy, the *Journal* said:[75]

---

[69] *Journal*, Sept. 16, 1896, 6.
[70] *Ibid.*, Oct. 16, 1896, 6.
[71] *Ibid.*, Nov. 24, 1896, 1.
[72] *Ibid.*, Nov. 13, 1896, 6.
[73] *Ibid.*, Nov. 16, 1896, 1.
[74] *Ibid.*, Nov. 18, 1896, 1.
[75] *Ibid.*, Nov. 28, 1896, 6.

> It is not at all improbable that events may happen, as General Johnson prophesies, and it is sure that if recognition of Cuban independence by this government means war, war we shall have, for it is inevitable that, sooner or later, the United States will declare itself the friend of Cuba.

The *Journal's* special correspondent in Madrid sent out dispatches dealing with Spain's alleged activity in war preparations.[76] One of the dispatches stated that "great activity continues in all Spanish ports, particularly in Cartagena, where the full available strength is now employed in fitting out six ironclads and three cruisers, which, with the Glasgow torpedo boat destroyers, will make a powerful flying squadron."[77]

In another article the newspaper asked, "Does Spain mean war?" charging that she was "stung to shame and blind rage" by the failure of Weyler to conquer the rebels and was intent on wreaking her vengeance on the United States.[78] The *Journal* argued that intervention would follow recognition of belligerency and that intervention would mean war.[79] Referring to the action of Congress in seeking to recognize Cuban belligerency, the Hearst paper stated that "Congress is acting in response to an irresistible pressure from the American people."

The *Journal* polled the United States senators as to their position with respect to the "passing of a joint resolution which shall be mandatory on the president to protect the struggling Cubans from being exterminated by the Spanish," and published favorable replies from fourteen senators.[80] Later, it polled the governors on the following questions: "First—do you favor on the part of the United States such interference in the Cuban revolution, by recognition or by the giving of material aid, as would promote the war for independence; second—how many volunteers would your state probably furnish for the sea and land forces respectively in case of war with a foreign power?"[81]

---

76 *Cf. ibid.*, December, 1896.
77 *Ibid.*, Dec. 1, 1896, 1.
78 *Ibid.*, Dec. 5, 1896, 6.
79 *Ibid.*, Dec. 19, 1896, 6.
80 *Ibid.*, Nov. 25, 1896, 1.
81 *Ibid.*, Dec. 18, 1896, 1.

The newspaper received favorable replies from twenty-five officials and the number of men they proposed to furnish in case of war ranged from 2,000 to 25,000. Two days later, the *Journal* published statements from a large group of senators criticizing Cleveland for his attitude toward the Cuban question.[82]

After Creelman went to Madrid as the *Journal* correspondent in 1897, news articles, telling about the feeling in Spain toward the United States, appeared frequently in the Hearst paper.[83] One of these dispatches the *Journal* displayed on the front page under the headline, "Crisis in Spain Almost at Hand; Whole Nation Is Thrilled with an Overpowering Sense of Impending Disaster." Discussing the situation in Spain, the newspaper said that the nation was about bankrupt and that "she can neither prosecute a war of the first class, nor even long maintain her strife against Cuban patriots."[84] The *Journal* carried another news article written by Representative Money of Mississippi, a member of the Committee on Foreign Affairs, following a tour he had made of the island, in which he was quoted as saying that Spain could never conquer Cuba.[85]

Both of the major political parties in 1896 had adopted planks in their platforms expressing a friendly feeling for Cuba and a desire to see the rebellion ended.[86] After the election of McKinley in November, 1896, the *Journal* said that the "next president has a fine opportunity to set the United States right before all nations and give them an example in the treatment of bullies that should result in the settlement of 'the Eastern Question.' " The *Journal* carried what it termed the "first statement of McKinley's Cuban policy" in February, 1897, in which the President-elect made it plain that "there will not be any meddling with the Cuban insurrection or any trifling with Spain."[87] When it became evident that the policy of McKinley was not to be radically different from that of Cleveland, the Hearst paper turned its attack upon him, charging that he was being influenced by "Wall Street."[88]

---

[82] *Ibid.*, Dec. 20, 1896, 2.
[83] *Ibid.*, Jan. 3, 1897, 1.
[84] *Ibid.*, Jan. 4, 1897, 6.
[85] *Ibid.*, Jan. 11, 1897, 1.
[86] *Ibid.*, Nov. 4, 1896, 6.
[87] *Ibid.*, Feb. 26, 1897, 1.
[88] *Ibid.*, July 26, 1897, 6.

When the Senate Foreign Relations Committee acted favorably upon one of the many resolutions introduced in Congress dealing with Cuban belligerency, the *Journal* with a headline completely across a page proclaimed: "Senators Declare for War with Spain" and "A Vote Shows the Senate Is Overwhelmingly Opposed to the Administration's Supine Policy."[89] In arguing for favorable action by the United States toward Cuba, it pointed out that the congressional elections were not far distant and that the Republicans should turn their minds toward trying to win these. If McKinley continued the Cleveland policy, the Hearst paper stated, the Republicans need not expect much support from the people:[90]

> It has been revealed that a protective tariff no longer inspires the masses with enthusiasm, and it is with agonies of apprehension that the party looks forward to the necessity of dealing with finances. The need for popularity will press imperiously upon the party presently and President McKinley is experienced enough as a gauger of public feeling to know that an utter abandonment of the pro-Spanish policy which he has inherited from the Cleveland administration would be warmly approved by the people.

The *Journal* opened its columns to Cuban sympathizers, particularly senators and representatives.[91] Senators Morgan of Alabama and Allen of Nebraska wrote letters to the paper in which the former stated that if he were president he "would bombard Havana" and the latter said that "our flag should protect citizens."[92]

The war which broke out in 1897 between Turkey and Greece for a short time completely overshadowed the Cuban conflict during which period the *Journal* carried little Cuban news.

McKinley called Congress into extra session in May, 1897, to deal with the tariff question, but many senators and representatives "harped on" the Cuban situation.[93] When the Senate voted for recognition of Cuban belligerency, the *Journal* stated that the "Senate declares that war in Cuba

---

[89] *Ibid.*, Feb. 26, 1897, 3.
[90] *Ibid.*, March 14, 1897, 6.
[91] *Cf. ibid.*, March, 1897.
[92] *Ibid.*, March 12, 1897, 2.
[93] *Ibid.*, May 21, 1897, 1.

does exist'' and that favorable action in the House was barred by ''Czar Reed's iron rule.'' American intervention in Cuba, the newspaper said, was demanded by ''every consideration of common interest, decency, and humanity.''[94] In criticizing the policy of McKinley, the Hearst paper stated that he would ''recognize Cuban independence to divert the mind of the public from the misery caused by the tariff bill when it is passed.''[95] Despite the exhortations of the *Journal,* however, Congress adjourned in July without settling the Cuban question.[96] Following the assassination of Premier Canavos, which it asserted meant the freeing of Cuba, the *Journal* for a short time abated its campaign for the Cuban cause.[97]

The news policy of the Boston *Herald* was in sharp contrast to its editorial policy. While news of Cuban affairs was ''played up,'' the editorials of the paper advocated a much more conservative policy with respect to the granting of belligerency rights than other papers previously considered. Backing the policy of President Cleveland and Secretary Olney, the *Herald* did not favor annexation of Cuba but rather advocated its purchase if the United States could get Spain to sell the island for $50,000,000 or $75,000,000.[98] It opposed war with Spain and any interference in Cuba, contending that ''we are not called upon to play a chivalrous rival to Spain.''[99] Admitting that there was much sympathy in this country for the rebels, the Boston paper attributed a great deal of the ''hysterics of indignation'' to professional politicians who ''join in it as they do in a good many things, because they think it will gain votes for them and their party.''[100] After Weyler's ''Reconcentrado'' program was well under way, the *Herald* changed its editorial policy to some extent and assumed a more sympathetic attitude toward the Cuban cause.[101] Evidently influenced in its news policy by the *World* and *Journal,* which were offering considerable competition, the *Herald* allotted generous space to Cuban news, particularly reports of debates in Congress dealing with recognition. In one news dispatch from Wash-

[94] *Ibid.,* May 24, 1897, 6.
[95] *Ibid.,* June 8, 1897, 2.
[96] *Ibid.,* July 26, 1897, 6.
[97] *Ibid.,* Aug. 10, 1897, 1.
[98] Boston *Herald,* Oct. 19, 1895, 6.
[99] *Ibid.,* Nov. 14, 1896, 6.
[100] *Ibid.,* April 14, 1896, 6.
[101] *Ibid.,* Aug. 28, 1896, 6.

ington, the Boston paper stated that "Uncle Sam" might give the patriots of Cuba freedom "as a Christmas present,"[102] and a few days later, in referring to Consul-General Lee's report to the President, the *Herald* said that "Cuba is sure to be free."[103] Lee later came to be *persona non grata,* the *Herald* said, because he "advised the president to aid the Cubans."[104] When General Maceo, rebel leader, lost his life in Cuba late in 1896, the *Herald,* like many other newspapers, charged that he and his staff had been "lured to their death under cover of a flag of truce" by the Marquis Ahumada.[105]

President McKinley sent a commissioner to Cuba in May, 1897, to ascertain the condition of affairs there, and this move by the chief executive was the occasion for more discussion of the Cuban question.[106] The *Herald* asserted that American citizens were "said to be in great destitution there," and senators sympathetic toward the rebels made good use of these news reports in their debates on the Cuban situation.[107] When the President asked Congress on May 17 for $50,000 to aid several hundred destitute American citizens in Cuba, his action was regarded as proof of the authenticity of the news reports carried by the newspapers with respect to suffering in the island.[108] For several days following McKinley's request, there were bitter debates in Congress on resolutions dealing with the Cuban question delivered before crowded galleries.[109] Following an active day in Congress, the *Herald* said that the debates "stirred the galleries" and that a "glimpse of the skeletons in the state department closet was afforded."[110] During one of the debates, Senator Foraker of Ohio, so the *Herald* stated, was "forced to make some startling disclosures." The "startling disclosures" proved to be that "Spain had refused Mr. Olney's offer of this country's good offices in Cuba." There was also "bitter denunciation of that 'mad dog' Weyler."

Senator Morgan had introduced a resolution in the Senate, April 1, 1897, providing for recognition of the belligerency of

[102] *Ibid.,* Oct. 17, 1896, 1.
[103] *Ibid.,* Nov. 23, 1896, 1.
[104] *Ibid.,* Nov. 27, 1896, 1.
[105] *Ibid.,* Dec. 13, 1896, 1.
[106] *Ibid.,* May 12, 1897, 1.
[107] *Ibid.,* May 14, 1897, 1.
[108] *Ibid.,* May 18, 1897, 1.
[109] *Ibid.,* May 19, 1897, 1.
[110] *Ibid.,* May 20, 1897, 1.

the Cuban rebels, and this measure came up for final action on May 20.[111] For several hours a heated debate centered about the adoption of the measure during which Senator Elkins of West Virginia admitted that he had been influenced by newspaper reports when he voted for a similar resolution in February, 1896.[112] The Morgan resolution was approved by the Senate by a vote of 41 to 14, and the next day the *Herald* charged that "popular clamor, as voiced by the galleries, was said to have influenced the senators."[113]

President McKinley, however, declined to be influenced by congressional action on resolutions dealing with Cuba. In his annual message to Congress, Dec. 6, 1897, he refused recognition of belligerency, pointing out the advantage of such a policy to Spain, and in a special message to Congress early in 1898, the President stated that he saw no reason for changing his view.[114]

The Milwaukee *Sentinel,* while opposing recognition of belligerency, carried full reports of debates in Congress on measures dealing with the Cuban question.[115] The Cincinnati *Commercial-Gazette* also gave prominent display to congressional debates.[116]

Several of the leading periodicals published articles about Cuba. Among these were *The Forum* and the *North American Review,* which carried articles by Clarence King and Mayo W. Hazeltine, already referred to. The former magazine also used an article by Senator Henry Cabot Lodge, who advocated recognition of Cuban belligerency.[117] Apparently Senator Lodge was moved by economic reasons in urging recognition, for he pointed out the advantages that might come to the United States in maintaining close relations with the island:

> The danger to American property in Cuba, the ruin of American commerce, the immense field which would be opened to American enterprise, and the market which would be secured for American products by Cuban independence, as well as the enormous geo-

[111] *Cong. Rec.*, 55 Congress, 1 Sess., XXX, Pt. 2, 1186, May 20, 1897.
[112] *Ibid.*, 1173.
[113] Boston *Herald,* May 21, 1897, 1.
[114] 55 Congress, 2 Sess., *House Doc.* No. 405, 8.
[115] *Sentinel,* May 21, 1896, 4.
[116] *Commercial-Gazette,* March 13, 1896, 1.
[117] Henry Cabot Lodge, "Our Duty to Cuba" in *The Forum,* XXI, May, 1896, 286.

> graphical and political importance of the island—all are weighty reasons for decisive action on our part.

Senator Lodge contended that the rebels had established a well-functioning civil government.[118]

After reciting a brief history of Spanish rule in the island, King urged recognition of the Cuban rebels.[119] He asserted that Spain had already shown her inability to conquer Cuba in the "Ten Years' War" and that if the United States prevented the sending of munitions of war to Cuba and continued to allow Spain to buy ships and arms, this country, not Spain, would conquer Cuba.[120] In this statement, King was resorting to the same faulty arguments used by several newspapers, for belligerency rights would not have changed American relations with Cuba insofar as the sale and shipment of arms and ammunition were concerned. Evidently King was not so much interested in the granting of belligerency as he was in giving aid to the rebels:[121]

> Is it difficult for us to decide between free Cuba and tyrant Spain? Why not fling overboard Spain and give Cuba the aid which she needs and which our treaty with Spain cannot prevent? Which cause is morally right?—Which manly?—Which American?

The article by Hazeltine dealt largely with Cuban self-government, which he said was a myth.[122] Presenting arguments in favor of belligerency, he contended that not only was it the duty of the United States to recognize the Cubans but that such action would be in conformity with the traditional policy of this government:[123]

> . . . The frequent use in the newspapers of the term "infraction" of neutrality laws, as applied to filibustering expeditions, is misleading. The United States cannot be neutral, because they have not acknowledged the existence of a state of war in Cuba. If they had, the rights of belligerency would have followed as a matter of course.

---

118 *Ibid.*, 282.
119 King, *loc. cit.*, 55.
120 *Ibid.*, 60.
121 *Ibid.*, 65.
122 Hazeltine, *loc. cit.*, 407.
123 *Ibid.*, 411.

This argument of Hazeltine is deceptive. The neutrality acts of 1794 and 1818 are comprehensive, and would prevent the fitting out in this country of any hostile expedition against any nation with which the United States is at peace. Hazeltine should have pointed out that there were no restrictions imposed against the free passage of Cubans to and from this country and of American citizens to and from Cuba, nor were there any restrictions against the enlistment of Americans in the Cuban cause.

Leslie's Weekly, using arguments similar to those employed by sensational newspapers, from time to time advocated recognition of Cuban belligerency.[124]

The controversy over belligerency rights provided one of the livest issues that arose during the Cuban revolt. Almost every significant news story concerning the rebels served sensational newspapers with a text for an editorial on the subject of recognition. Some editorial writers showed little knowledge of the subject as indicated by the fallacious arguments used; others evidently misrepresented purposely the issues involved. As a result, newspaper readers were fed half truths, exaggerations, and misstatements of fact. That they were unable to form a sound opinion regarding the merits of the controversy is obvious.

Agitation for recognition of belligerency was continued by partisan newspapers, in a more or less persistent manner, until the Maine disaster occurred in February, 1898, after which events moved rapidly toward war with Spain.

---

[124] *Cf. Leslie's Weekly,* LXXXII.

CHAPTER VI

THE "NEW JOURNALISM"

The year 1897 marks definitely the beginning of what the New York *Journal* referred to as the "New Journalism"—a policy of aggressive activity in bringing to light unusual incidents which were exploited to build circulation. A good illustration of the *Journal's* attitude toward the "New Journalism" is seen in one of its cartoons showing "Uncle Sam" drinking to a youth, the *Journal,* while standing upon a huge stack of papers, representing circulation, with the word "Scoop" suspended from his body.[1] The *Journal* referred to its accomplishments in obtaining news as "the journalism that does things,"[2] and poked fun at its competitors for their lack of initiative.[3] Adopting the slogan, "While others talk the *Journal* acts," the Hearst paper frequently mentioned the "New Journalism," occasionally boasting of its growth in circulation.[4] Paraphrasing the New York *Sun* slogan, "If you see it in the *Sun* it's so," the *Journal* said: "If you see it in the Sun you're lucky."[5] Especially was it critical of Pulitzer and the *World.*[6] The influence of the Hearst paper on other newspapers is indicated by the way in which the latter "played up" news reports uncovered by the *Journal.*

A series of news events occurred during 1897 and early 1898, for which the *Journal* was either wholly or partly responsible, that obviously played a part in arousing public feeling against Spain. These were the Ruiz affair, the Cisneros rescue, and the De Lome letter.

Ricardo Ruiz was a Cuban dentist who had participated in the revolt of 1868-1878, after which he had come to this country, taken out naturalization papers, and returned to Cuba where he married and reared a family.[7] He was arrested on a charge of participating in a train robbery and was found dead in his prison cell. Immediately the *Journal* came out with the headline, "American Slain in Spanish Jail," and for days it carried news dispatches prominently displayed

---

1 *Journal,* July 5, 1897, 1.
2 *Ibid.,* Oct. 13, 1897, 8.
3 *Ibid.,* Oct. 11, 1897, 4.
4 *Ibid.,* March 24, 1897, 2.
5 *Ibid.,* April 14, 1897, 4.
6 *Ibid.,* Aug. 22, 1897, 6.
7 Boston *Herald,* March 3, 1897, 1.

concerning the affair.[8] The Hearst paper said that there was "strong evidence to show that the hapless man was murdered by a Spanish policeman in his cell," Two days later, with five-column headlines, the *Journal* announced: "Sherman for War with Spain for Murdering Americans."[9] Secretary Sherman was quoted as saying that he had no information concerning the death of Ruiz, save what he had read in the *Journal*. He was quoted further as stating that "if the facts are true, as reported, and American citizens are being murdered in Cuba in cold blood, the only way to put an end to the atrocities is to declare war on Spain."[10] The latter part of the statement was set in heavy type. The *Journal* then reported that Consul-General Lee had tendered his resignation because his demand for the protection of Americans had not been heeded.[11] It also carried a statement from Senator Chandler of New Hampshire demanding vigorous action on the part of the United States in protecting Americans and American interests in Cuba.

Contending that it had received a "message from Ruiz as from the grave," the *Journal* asserted that the "American dentist, murdered in Guanabacoa jail, scratched on the back of a steamer chair that he was being killed."[12] It added that he was tortured to death in his cell by Spanish jailors. When it was charged that Ruiz was not a naturalized American, the *Journal* printed a facsimile of his naturalization papers to prove that he had been naturalized.[13] After an investigation, the Spanish government reported that Ruiz had died from brain congestion, but this report was discounted by the Hearst paper, which stated that he was "murdered" and invariably when it referred to him it was as "the murdered American."[14]

The family of Ruiz, the Hearst paper asserted, was released from confinement in prison after his death through the "efforts of the *Journal*," following which Mrs. Ruiz wrote to the newspaper, telling how she had been wronged and thanking it for its efforts in her behalf.[15] The Journal used a whole page of pictures of Mrs. Ruiz in announcing that she

---

[8] *Journal*, Feb. 20, 1897, 1.
[9] *Ibid.*, Feb. 22, 1897, 1.
[10] *Ibid.*, Feb. 22, 1897, 1.
[11] *Ibid.*, Feb. 24, 1897, 2.
[12] *Ibid.*, Feb. 25, 1897, 1.
[13] *Ibid.*, Feb. 27, 1897, 5.
[14] *Ibid.*, Feb. 28, 1897, 4.
[15] *Ibid.*, March 6, 1897, 3.

was coming to the United States to file a claim against Spain.[16] Through the further "efforts of the *Journal*," Mrs. Ruiz visited Washington, obtained an audience with President McKinley, Secretary Sherman,[17] and with Rep. R. R. Hitt of Illinois, chairman of the Committee on Foreign Affairs, the latter informing her that Spain was "answerable for the dentist's death."[18] While in Washington, Mrs. Ruiz was invited to visit Rep. Charles Curtis of Kansas (later Vice-President of the United States), and a three-column picture showed Curtis holding "Baby" Gloria Ruiz in his arms.[19]

Action was taken by the Senate looking toward an investigation concerning the arrest, imprisonment, and death of Ruiz,[20] and Sherman "prodded" De Lome because of his delay in securing the release of "certain American prisoners still unlawfully held by the Spanish authorities in Cuba."[21] The *Journal* raised the question of the legality of Ruiz's imprisonment and quoted a professor of international law at Harvard university in an effort to show that Spain was violating the Protocol of 1877 and the Treaty of 1795 in dealing with Americans.[22] The *Journal* also interviewed members of Congress to determine their attitude in regard to the Ruiz affair: one senator suggested that the United States "send cannon if needed;" another said "send cruisers;" still another wanted an inquiry; and one favored reparations.[23]

The Chicago *Tribune* took up the Ruiz case, charging that "reputable newspaper correspondents, working independently, agree on the facts that this American has been ruthlessly murdered."[24] It also asserted that "in the case of Ruiz it seems that the torture was protracted for four days."[25]

The death of Ruiz was the occasion for sharp criticism by the New Orleans *Times-Democrat* of the administration's attitude toward Cuba and especially its reported failure to protect Americans in the island. Referring to the Ruiz affair, the *Times-Democrat* remarked:[26]

---

16 *Ibid.*, March 10, 1897, 15.
17 *Ibid.*, March 12, 1897, 1.
18 *Ibid.*, March 19, 1897, 3.
19 *Ibid.*, March 20, 1897, 1.
20 *Ibid.*, March 23, 1897, 1.
21 *Ibid.*, March 25, 1897, 4.
22 *Ibid.*, Feb. 14, 1897, 2.
23 *Ibid.*, Feb. 22, 1897, 2.
24 Chicago *Tribune*, Feb. 2, 1897, 28.
25 *Ibid.*, Feb. 25, 1897, 6.
26 *Times-Democrat*, Feb. 23, 1897, 4.

> There appears to be not a suspicion of doubt but that the death in prison of Dr. Ruiz, an American citizen, and one who practiced his profession of dentistry in Cuba without taking any part whatever in politics, was a murder of an unusually foul kind. Thrown into prison without reason and without so much as a notification to his friends, he lay in jail for twelve days; and at the end of that time, unless all signs prove deceptive, he was brutally beaten to death with clubs in his cell.
>
> If American citizens are to be imprisoned in Cuba without specific charge, kept in prison without trial, and then foully butchered as Dr. Ruiz appears to have been as a culmination of their illegal and unjust treatment, the only way, as Senator Sherman says, to negotiate with Spain over that sort of business, is to declare war against her.

The New Orleans paper added that Americans wanted Consul-General Lee backed up in his defense of American lives and American interests and American honor with a squadron of "Uncle Sam's" navy in the harbor of Havana.[27]

The New York *Sun* stated that Ruiz met his death under suspicious and horrible circumstances, which had aroused "deep feeling in the United States,"[28] and the Boston *Herald* reported that Lee had asked for a warship to avenge the death of Ruiz.[29] The Boston paper contended that the dentist's death was an outrage on American citizenship and that Secretary Olney had ordered a searching inquiry. Apparently affected by newspaper agitation of the Ruiz case, the Senate requested the President to protest against the trial of a "naturalized American" in Cuba, which the *Herald* said would be conducted by a "drum-head" court martial.[30]

The Indianapolis *Journal* used the Associated Press stories of the Ruiz case, which were evidently taken largely from the New York *World* reports,[31] and the San Francisco *Chronicle,* in addition to the Associated Press dispatches, used both the New York *Herald* and *Sun* services.[32] The Chi-

---

[27] *Ibid.,* Feb. 25, 1897, 4.
[28] *Sun,* Feb. 25, 1897, 6.
[29] *Herald,* Feb. 21, 1897, 1.
[30] *Ibid.,* April 6, 1897, 1.
[31] Indianapolis *Journal,* Feb. 22, 1897, 2.
[32] *Chronicle,* Feb. 23, 1897, 1.

cago *Times-Herald* asserted that Ruiz had been murdered in his cell and that his death led Lee to call for battleships to avert a crisis.[33] In prominent display, it stated that "Spain Must Answer for the Ruiz Outrage."[34] The *Times-Herald* also stated that the United States would demand indemnity from Spain for Ruiz's widow, but whether or not such payment was made by the Spanish government was not recorded by the press.[35]

The Cisneros rescue is perhaps one of the most notable instances of newspaper aggressiveness in history. Evangelina Cisneros, a niece of the Cuban President, Cisneros y Betancourt, who headed the civil government of the rebels, was charged with having lured Colonel Berris, Military Governor of the Isle of Pines, to her home where hidden men killed him. The Hearst paper, however, contended that Miss Cisneros was the most beautiful girl in all Cuba and that her innocence and beauty had "excited the lust" of the Governor, who was the nephew of the Prime Minister of Spain. Colonel Berris, according to the *Journal* account, offered protection to her father at the price of her honor, but Miss Cisneros "turned from the brute in horror and told her friends," who planned his death. She was convicted of sedition by a Spanish court martial and it was reported that she was in imminent danger of being sent to Spain's "African penal settlement for twenty years."[36] The newspaper championed her cause, securing the aid of hundreds of prominent women throughout the country.[37] Among these were Mrs. Jefferson Davis, who appealed to the Queen Regent of Spain in behalf of the prisoner, and Julia Ward Howe, who sought aid for Miss Cisneros from Pope Leo XIII.[38] Others who joined the Journal's fight included Mrs. John Sherman, Clara Barton, Mrs. John D. Logan, Mrs. Mark Hanna, and Mrs. E.D.E.N. Southworth, the novelist.[39] The *Journal* asserted that never before had there been witnessed such an uprising of women for a fellow woman. Referring to the case editorially, it said:[40]

---

[33] *Times-Herald*, Feb. 20, 1897, 1.
[34] *Ibid.*, Feb. 22, 1897, 1.
[35] *Ibid.*, June 9, 1897, 1.
[36] *Journal*, Aug. 17, 1897, 1.
[37] *Ibid.*, Aug. 22, 1897, 59.
[38] *Ibid.*, Aug. 19, 1897, 1.
[39] *Ibid.*, Aug. 22, 1897, 59.
[40] *Ibid.*, Aug. 19, 1897, 6.

> At last the ruffians who rule Cuba in the name of Spain have gone too far. They have roused America from its apathy, and have begun to reach such human feeling as exists in Spain itself. . . . In Washington and Havana the excitement aroused by the *Journal's* recital of the infamy perpetrated against Senorita Cisneros is so great that the Spanish authorities are alarmed, and are appealing to the bestial commandant to withdraw his charge.
>
> For the sake of the poor girl it is to be hoped that these varied efforts may prove successful. But if they should fail the unnatural alliance between our government and the barbarians who are devastating Cuba would be ended, and the Cuban republic would date its independence from the martyrdom of Evangelina Cisneros.

The *Journal* severely criticized the New York *World* for publishing a statement from Weyler, giving his account of the charges against Miss Cisneros,[41] and declared that the "women of America will save her yet in spite of Weyler and the *World*," for more than 10,000 women in all parts of the United States had signed a petition to the Queen Regent for her release.[42] The newspaper gave a list of names by states of women petitioning the Queen Regent, which filled twelve newspaper columns.[43] The New York clergy, the *Journal* stated, spoke in behalf of "Weyler's victim."[44]

Following the case day by day, the *Journal* carried accounts of the "girl's wrongs" as told by Miss Cisneros herself, and elaborated these by editorial comment. It quoted the girl as saying that she had acted in defense of her honor, and pictured her as having lain for nine months in a prison "threatened by consumption." The newspaper referred to Miss Cisneros as being "in death's shadow," racked by the pain of terrible suffering. With five-column pictures, it showed Miss Cisneros as she was when arrested and as she appeared after nine months of prison life. The "pictures" were pen sketches and the first made Miss Cisneros appear as a beautiful young girl, while the latter

41 *Ibid.*, Aug. 22, 1897, 64.
42 *Ibid.*, Aug. 23, 1897, 1.
43 *Ibid.*, 2.
44 *Ibid.*, 3.

depicted her as wan and emaciated. The *Journal* emphasized that the "horrors of Weyler's warfare on Cuban women and children increase day by day."[45]

Announcing that "Mother" McKinley, wife of the President, had lent her voice in behalf of Miss Cisneros, the Hearst paper quoted her as saying that she was in sympathy with the *Journal's* move to secure the girl's release.[46] The newspaper printed a "Roll of Honor" containing the names of "notable women who will aid in securing liberty for the fair Cuban."[47] The list included the names, in addition to those already mentioned, of such prominent women as Mrs. William C. Whitney, wife of the former Secretary of the Navy; Mrs. John G. Carlysle, wife of the former Secretary of the Treasury; Miss Eugenia Washington, grandniece of George Washington; and Mrs. Letitia Tyler Semple, daughter of President Tyler.[48]

The *Journal* also published "pictures" of the "vilest prison of Cuba" where Miss Cisneros was held, and in editorials enlarged upon these alleged conditions and the cruelties shown Miss Cisneros.[49] It stated that the "truth is too black to be hidden" and that the girl was a "martyr to Spanish brutality."[50]

While working in behalf of Miss Cisneros, the *Journal* interpreted news events as showing that a conflict with Spain was imminent.[51] It reported that preparations for war were being made and asked: "Are we going to fight?"[52] The following day, it announced that De Lome's naval attache was inspecting forts in the United States,[53] and that "with the help of the *Journal*" the United States government had been enabled to identify the Spanish spy who had been secretly informing himself of this country's Atlantic coast defenses.[54] Comparing Spain's navy with that of the United States, the Hearst paper asserted that it would be futile for the former to match her force with that of this country.[55] According to the *Journal,* the United States was taking severe measures to end the Cuban trouble, and plans were being made rapidly

[45] *Ibid.*, Aug. 20, 1897, 6.
[46] *Ibid.*, Aug. 24, 1897, 1.
[47] *Ibid.*, Aug. 23, 1897, 2.
[48] *Cf. ibid.*, Aug. 23, 1897, 2.
[49] *Ibid.*, Aug. 24, 1897, 6.
[50] *Cf. ibid.*, Aug. 24-31, 1897.
[51] *Ibid.*, Aug. 28, 1897, 6.
[52] *Ibid.*, Sept. 9, 1897, 6.
[53] *Ibid.*, Sept. 10, 1897, 1.
[54] *Ibid.*, Sept. 11, 1897, 6.
[55] *Ibid.*, Sept. 13, 1897, 6.

for war.[56] The newspaper quoted *Le Temps* of Paris as stating that war seemed imminent, and added that *Le Temps* was a reliable newspaper.[57] A half-page cartoon, depicting a huge American eagle perched upon guns defying Weyler to attack women and children under its wings, was used on its front page, all of which was devoted to Cuban news.[58] Asserting that McKinley had set November 1 as the date on which Spain must bring the Cuban conflict to a close, the *Journal* said that "the Rubicon has been crossed" and that the United States had intervened to put an end to "the barbarous war which for two years has drenched Cuba with patriotic blood and laid waste the island."[59] Since the United States had taken the "irrevocable step," the Hearst paper said, everything possible would be done to place this country on a strong war footing.[60] There is no evidence to support these statements, which evidently originated in the imagination of a member of the *Journal* staff.

After hinting that Miss Cisneros would be rescued, the newspaper with striking headlines, announced that she had been delivered from her prison by the *Journal* and was on her way to the United States.[61] A *Journal* correspondent, Karl Decker, had succeeded in spiriting Miss Cisneros from her prison disguised as a boy and in placing her aboard a vessel bound for New York.[62] For several days Hearst's paper exploited the event, devoting the larger part of its issues to a recital of how the rescue was achieved and the way it was received by the women of the United States.[63] Recounting how Miss Cisneros was taken from "Weyler's prison at the dead of night by *Journal* correspondents at the peril of their lives,"[64] the newspaper asserted that it had promised the women of the United States that Miss Cisneros should be free and that it had kept its promise.[65] When it was suggested that international complications might result from the Cisneros rescue, the *Journal* quoted Elihu Root as saying that this country was not responsible for what the res-

---

[56] *Ibid.*, Sept. 14, 1897, 1.
[57] *Ibid.*, Sept. 21, 1897, 1.
[58] *Ibid.*, Sept. 22, 1897, 1.
[59] *Ibid.*, Sept. 23, 1897, 8.
[60] *Ibid.*, Sept. 24, 1897, 6.
[61] *Ibid.*, Oct. 9, 1897, 1.
[62] *Ibid.*, Oct. 15, 1897, 1.
[63] *Cf. ibid.*, Oct. 11-23, 1897.
[64] *Ibid.*, Oct. 11, 1897, 3, 6.
[65] *Ibid.*, Oct. 12, 1897, 1.

cuers did.[66] The Hearst paper boasted of its achievement, claiming that "statesmen, tailors, women and people in every walk of life" were lauding its rescue, and numerous persons were quoted to show that Americans everywhere were pleased. Secretary Sherman was reported as stating that "everyone would sympathize with the *Journal's* enterprise in releasing Miss Cisneros,"[67] and McKinley was quoted to the effect that Sherman's statement "correctly voiced the unofficial sentiment of the administration.[68] Praise from everywhere came to the *Journal* and even Europe, it asserted, was stirred by the "heroic act."[69]

Not satisfied merely with rescuing Miss Cisneros, the *Journal* arranged a reception for her in Union Square, New York City,[70] gave a reception in her honor in the *Journal* building, and took her to Washington to see McKinley.[71] In a large front-page picture the *Journal* showed Miss Cisneros shaking hands with the President.

Newspapers all over the country used the Associated Press dispatches telling of the *Journal's* rescue of Miss Cisneros.[72] A news dispatch carried by the Indianapolis *Journal* said that Washington "is mightily stirred up over the liberation of Miss Cisneros," and that the rescue was one of the most "daring feats ever attempted and successfully carried out."[73] Decker's account of the rescue, as sent out by the Associated Press, was given prominent display by member papers.[74] In addition to carrying accounts of the rescue, the Chicago *Tribune* published pictures of Miss Cisneros, which it secured from the New York *Journal*.[75] Thus, through the enterprise of the New York *Journal* and the co-operation of the Associated Press, newspaper readers in all parts of the United States were furnished accounts of the rescue of the Cuban girl.

An incident occurred in February, 1898 that directly affected diplomatic relations between the United States and Spain and probably contributed more than any single event,

---

66 *Ibid.*, 8, 9.
67 *Ibid.*, Oct. 11, 1897, 1.
68 *Ibid.*, Oct. 13, 1897, 1.
69 *Ibid.*, Oct. 13, 1897, 2, 3.
70 *Ibid.*, Oct. 14, 1897, 6.
71 *Ibid.*, Oct. 16, 1897, 1.
72 *Cf.* Charleston *News and Courier*, Oct. 13, 1897, 1; Indianapolis *Journal*, Oct. 12, 1897, 1; New Orleans *Times-Democrat*, Oct. 9, 1897, 1; San Francisco *Chronicle*, Oct. 10, 1897, 1.
73 Indianapolis *Journal*, Oct. 12, 1897, 1.
74 *Cf. Times-Democrat*, Oct. 14, 1897, 1; *Chronicle*, Oct. 14, 1897, 1.
75 Chicago *Tribune*, Oct. 14, 1897, 1.

prior to the sinking of the battleship Maine, toward causing opposition to Spain. This episode was the publication by the New York *Journal* of the De Lome letter, written by Dupuy De Lome to Jose Canalejas y Mendez, editor of *El Heraldo de Madrid,* in which the Spanish Minister called McKinley a "low politician catering to the rabble."[76] The letter was addressed to Canalejas at Havana where he was on a mission for Spain and was stolen, apparently by a member of the Cuban Junta, and given to the *Journal,* which devoted all of its front page and more to the incident. It was another *Journal* "scoop."[77] The newspaper claimed that a man risked his life to get the letter, which was taken from Canalejas's desk in Havana without his ever knowing that it was stolen.[78] There were different newspaper versions, however, as to the manner in which the letter was stolen.[79] The reference to President McKinley was as follows:[80]

> Besides the natural and inevitable coarseness with which he (McKinley) repeats all that the press and public opinion of Spain has said of Weyler, it shows once more that McKinley is—weak and catering to the rabble, and, besides, a low politician, who desires to leave a door open to me and to stand well with the jingoes of his party.

De Lome in his letter also attacked the *Journal* correspondent at Havana for the sensational news stories which he was charged with dispatching to his paper.[81]

At first there was a tendency on the part of American officials to doubt the authenticity of the letter, but the *Journal* published a facsimile of the communication, the handwriting of which it compared with other letters written by De Lome.[82] The Spanish Minister later acknowledged that he was the author of the letter.[83] General Woodford, American Minister at Madrid, was instructed to get immediately an answer from Sagasta, the Spanish Prime Minister, to the demand for instant action by the Spanish government.[84]

---

[76] *Cf. Journal,* Feb. 9, 1898, 1.
[77] *Ibid.,* 6.
[78] *Ibid.,* Feb. 10, 1898, 2.
[79] *Times-Democrat,* Feb. 14, 1898, 1.
[80] *Journal,* Feb. 9, 1898, 1.
[81] *Idem.*
[82] Milwaukee *Sentinel,* Feb. 10, 1898, 1.
[83] New York *Sun,* Feb. 10, 1898, 1.
[84] *World,* Feb. 10, 1898, 1.

The De Lome episode was compared by the newspapers to that of Lord Sackville-West, British Minister to the United States, who was dismissed after he admitted writing a letter to a recently naturalized American citizen of British birth in reply to the latter's request for guidance as to how to vote in the presidential election of 1888, and it was generally agreed that De Lome should be dismissed at once.[85]

The *Journal* asserted that "from this episode may grow war," because the President could not overlook the "offense."[86] It referred to De Lome's statement criticizing American women which he was reported to have made in a book, "From Madrid to Madrid," written several years previously, as showing that this was not his first offense. The Hearst paper insisted that the Minister be dismissed, and when it was announced that Woodford would inform Spain that De Lome was *persona non grata,* the *Journal* boasted that it had "fixed his guilt."[87] A cartoon drawn by Homer Davenport, one of Hearst's best known cartoonists, appeared in the *Journal* showing an angry and impatient "Uncle Sam" pointing to the door of the White House with the single word to De Lome, "Git."[88] For several days the *Journal* "played up" the event, and in its editorial comment it denounced De Lome and Spain and urged that the Minister should be dismissed peremptorily:[89]

> Now let us have action immediate and decisive. The flag of Cuba Libre ought to float over Morro Castle within a week.

The New York *World* also advocated that De Lome immediately should be dismissed, and it carried a four-column cartoon showing "Uncle Sam" grasping the Spanish Minister by the nape of the neck and the seat of the pants with the words, "Now Walk Spanish."[90] Discussing the incident editorially, the *World* commented:[91]

> He (De Lome) has been guilty of an act outrageous and insulting to the country in any case, and peculiarly outrageous and insulting at a time when relations be-

[85] *Sentinel,* Feb. 10, 1898, 1.
[86] *Journal,* Feb. 8, 1898, 2.
[87] *Ibid.,* Feb. 10, 1898, 1.
[88] *Ibid.,* 4.
[89] *Ibid.,* Feb. 11, 1898, 6.
[90] *World,* Feb. 10, 1898, 1.
[91] *Ibid.,* 6.

> tween the two countries are strained almost to the breaking point.
>
> There will be a "disavowal" by the Madrid government, of course. That is polite diplomatic lingo for lying. It ought not to suffice. Until Dupuy De Lome is punished and assurances are given that his successor will behave like a gentleman, we should receive no successor to him. We at least can get on without any Spanish Minister at Washington.

The *World* also contended that this was not De Lome's first offense, referring to the book in which he was alleged to have made derogatory remarks about American women, and to the fact that in 1896 he had publicly criticized debate in the Senate on a Cuban resolution. Concerning the former charge, the *World* said:[92]

> He (De Lome) suggested in terms too plain to be misunderstood that American women were dissolute before marriage and after, and that after marriage they earned in disreputable ways the money they spent in foreign travel and the like.
>
> The blistering disgrace of all this thing is that a man who has so grievously traduced and slandered American women has been received six years as minister!
>
> An administration with blood in its veins and iron in its blood would have regarded the reputation of American womankind as immeasurably of more importance than the reputation of a president. Such an administration would have given this slanderer his "Carge" (*sic*) long ago.

The contents of the De Lome letter were sent by the Associated Press to member papers, which "played up" the incident.[93] Several of the publications also received additional news reports concerning the episode through their special news services.[94]

The New York *Sun,* in discussing the incident, remarked that "it is well that Mr. De Lome, being caught in the per-

[92] *Idem.*
[93] *Cf. Times-Democrat,* Indianapolis *Journal,* Milwaukee *Sentinel,* San Francisco *Chronicle,* Feb. 10, 1898.
[94] *Cf. Chronicle, Times-Democrat,* Indianapolis *Journal,* Feb. 10, 1898.

petration of the insult to the country, should be driven from his post as the Spanish Minister in Washington,'"[95] and the *Chronicle* asserted that "his usefulness at Washington being at an end, his further stay there would be a waste of time.'"[96] The Indianapolis *Journal* commented that "it is not probable that the De Lome incident will lead to war with Spain but it is possible.'"[97] Not only had De Lome by this letter wrecked his career as a diplomatist, the Chicago *Times-Herald* said, but he had "exposed the machiavelian hypocrisy of Spain in her intercourse with other countries.'"[98] The Chicago *Tribune* received accounts of the De Lome episode from its Washington bureau, which it was maintaining at this time, in addition to the regular Associated Press reports.[99] Asserting that the incident might mean war, this newspaper said that the "President of the United States cannot receive an insult of so flagrant a nature from Spain without resenting it.'"[100]

Immediately following publication of the De Lome letter, a resolution, introduced by Senator Morgan of Alabama, was adopted by the Senate requesting the President to send to that body copies of the reports of the Consul-General in Cuba received by the State Department since March 4, 1897.[101] The publication of the letter was also the occasion for debate in the Senate on several resolutions introduced previous to the De Lome incident,[102] with reference to which action the San Francisco *Chronicle* said that the galleries of Congress were packed with people "who were aware that this would be a field day for Cuban oratory,'"[103] and the Indianapolis *Journal* remarked:[104]

> The two inflammatory speeches which were made in the Senate today by Senators Cannon and Mason are regarded as most dangerous contributions to an already over-strained situation.

The De Lome incident created a sensation in Washington, New York and Chicago,[105] and interest in the debates on

---

[95] *Sun,* Feb. 17, 1898, 6.
[96] *Chronicle,* Feb. 10, 1898, 6.
[97] *Journal,* Feb. 11, 1898, 4.
[98] *Times-Herald,* Feb. 11, 1898, 6.
[99] *Tribune,* Feb. 11, 1898, 1.
[100] *Ibid.,* Feb. 12, 1898, 4.
[101] *Cong. Rec.,* 55 Congress, 2 Sess., XXXI, Pt. 2, 1679, Feb. 14, 1898.
[102] *Ibid.,* 1682.
[103] San Francisco *Chronicle,* Feb. 10, 1898, 1.
[104] Indianapolis *Journal,* Feb. 10, 1898, 1.
[105] New York *World,* Feb. 9, 1898, 1.

Cuban belligerency was replaced by a discussion of the letter.[106]

De Lome was not dismissed by the government of the United States for he resigned two days after the letter was published, and his resignation was accepted by the Spanish government, much to the "chagrin of the administration."[107] The Spanish government, however, apologized for the letter, and disavowed the statements made by the Minister.[108]

The New York *Journal,* scenting war in the De Lome incident, began playing up a "war scare" with "banner" headlines.[109] About this time the Hearst paper was carrying a series of atrocity stories written by Julian Hawthorne, which was largely a repetition of what both it and the *World* had already published about starving Cubans.[110]

The De Lome incident was discussed in the pulpit, and when one New York minister referred to the "insult," his congregation shouted: "Let us get at the Spaniards! Let there be war! Down with the woman slayers!"[111]

The De Lome episode obviously intensified popular feeling in the United States against Spain.[112] Filibusters increased their activities and as one militant Cuban said: "The De Lome letter is a great thing for us."[113]

The wide publicity given these news events by the press could produce only one result—greater opposition to Spanish rule in Cuba and deeper sympathy for the rebels. The primary appeal made by sensational newspapers in the death of Ruiz was Spain's disregard for the rights of American citizens, an appeal resorted to again and again throughout the period of the revolt. The Ruiz case was typical of the practice referred to of Cubans coming to this country, taking out naturalization papers and returning to the island, protected by American citizenship, to resume their struggle against the Spanish government. The case also offered opportunities for the press to harp on a question that has done as much perhaps as any other to raise diplomatic controversies between nations—the protection of citizenship.

---

[106] Chicago *Tribune,* Feb. 11, 1898, 6.
[107] *World,* Feb. 11, 1898, 1.
[108] *Ibid.,* Feb. 15, 1898, 2.
[109] New York *Journal,* Feb. 12, 1898, 1.
[110] *Ibid.,* Feb. 14, 1898, 34, 35.
[111] *Ibid.,* 2.
[112] *World,* Feb. 26, 1898, 6.
[113] *Ibid.,* Feb. 15, 1898, 2.

The Cisneros rescue combined the elements needed to make a sensational story, and interest in the event must have been widespread. The danger of international complications was evidently not considered by the Hearst paper, and the general acclaim that followed the rescue indicates the attitude of the American people in the matter.

The publication of the De Lome letter, following closely the Ruiz case and the Cisneros rescue, furnished additional fuel to feed the flame of American indignation toward Spain. The press could have relieved a tense situation by explaining that the communication was a private letter written to a private individual, the contents of which were disclosed by surreptitious means. Instead, with large headlines newspapers demanded the Minister's dismissal. Public opinion was quick to assert itself, but President McKinley did not act promptly enough and, much to the disappointment of several sensational journals, De Lome was permitted by Madrid to resign.

The American public had no other source of information concerning these incidents except what was revealed by the press. Inasmuch as those papers which devoted space to the events at all generally exaggerated the facts, and inasmuch as the nature of the news reports was such as to produce response, it seems evident that the feeling against Spain was intensified.

These three episodes, for which the sensational press was largely responsible, were agitated at a time when the relations between the United States and Spain were growing more strained each day and provided the proper psychological setting for the climax to the demand for American intervention in Cuba which was produced in the Maine disaster.

CHAPTER VII

THE MAINE DISASTER

Spain discussed a plan of autonomy for the Cubans as early as 1896, but she adhered to her policy to grant no reforms until after the rebels had laid down their arms.[1] The suggestion of reforms was opposed by a group of newspapers in this country on the grounds that Spain was insincere and was only using this proposal as a means of getting the Cubans to cease fighting.[2] The contention was also made that it was too late for Spain to consider home rule as Cuba was already lost to her.[3]

A decree, authorizing the proposed reforms, was signed early in 1897 by the Queen Regent of Spain, but the Cubans, backed by the American press which referred to the proposal as "sham reforms" deliberately designed to deceive the people in this country, refused to accept the terms laid down.[4] The plan was designated by the New York *Sun* as "Spain's new scheme to fool the Cubans."[5] The New Orleans *Times-Democrat* commented that the proposed reforms were hardly worth considering,[6] and the Chicago *Tribune* said that they "seemed to include everything except what Cuba wanted."[7]

After the Liberal party came into power in Spain in the fall of 1897, the proposal of reforms for Cuba was again made by Spain, but this time it was received with as much disfavor as the previous offers, despite the avowal of the Spanish government that it was sincere.[8] General Gomez announced that the Cubans would accept neither home rule nor any other kind of reform.[9] Again it was charged that the project had been launched chiefly for consumption in the United States and was to be regarded as a "makeshift and a device for gaining time."[10]

---

1 Boston *Herald,* Dec. 5, 1896, 1.
2 *World,* March 21, 1896, 6; *ibid.,* April 14, 1896, 7; *ibid.,* April 16, 1896, 6; Chicago *Tribune,* April 25, 1896, 12; New York *Sun,* May 11, 1896, 6.
3 New York *Sun,* May 11, 1896, 6; Chicago *Tribune,* Sept. 8, 1896, 6.
4 *Sun,* Feb. 5, 1897, 6.
5 *Ibid.,* Feb. 8, 1897, 6.
6 New Orleans *Times-Democrat,* Feb. 5, 1897, 4.
7 *Tribune,* Feb. 6, 1897, 12.
8 Boston *Herald,* Oct. 8, 1897, 6; *Review of Reviews,* XVI, December, 1897, 646.
9 *World,* Jan. 2, 1897, 1.
10 *Review of Reviews,* XVII, January, 1898, 131.

The New York *Journal* not only opposed autonomy, but demanded that Spain grant independence to Cuba.[11] Following its usual policy of seeing war in almost every move made by Spain, it asserted that the Spaniards were trying to force a conflict with the United States and that the latter, "on the eve of war," was busily engaged in strengthening its coast defenses and its navy,[12] To prove this assertion, the *Journal* announced that Theodore Roosevelt, Assistant Secretary of the Navy, had demanded more battleships, which were to be used to repel a Spanish invasion.[13]

President McKinley asked Congress to delay action on the Cuban question for one year to test the ability of Spain to put the proposed reforms into effect and to judge the efficiency of the changes,[14] but the *Journal* objected to this delay, and referred to the platform on which the President was elected as representing American opinion.[15]

The Westminster *Gazette* charged that the Hearst paper planned an invasion of Cuba, and the *Journal,* obviously pleased with the suggestion, boasted that "Spain fears the *Journal* and Karl Decker."[16] A few days later, the *Journal* news bureau in the American Consulate building in Havana was obliged to abandon its offices after repeated attempts had been made to dynamite the correspondents' quarters.[17]

The Spanish government definitely granted autonomy, Nov. 25, 1897, but Constitutional Unionists in Cuba and rebels alike rejected the proffered reforms. Attempts to inaugurate the new plan on Jan. 1, 1898, were met with vigorous resistance, and riots broke out in Havana.[18] The cause of the rioting was primarily attributed to a group of Spanish officers who were incensed at articles appearing in three Havana newspapers, one of which was opposed to Weyler.[19] The officers objected to denunciations of the Spanish government, and, when they were joined by a mob, they turned the protest into an anti-autonomistic affair.[20] The three newspaper offices were wrecked by the rioters, and the city was

---

[11] *Journal,* Nov. 16, 1897, 11.
[12] *Ibid.,* Nov. 8, 1897, 11.
[13] *Ibid.,* 4.
[14] *Ibid.,* Dec. 4, 1897, 8.
[15] *Ibid.,* Dec. 7, 1897, 6.
[16] *Ibid.,* Dec. 4, 1897, 1.
[17] *Ibid.,* Dec. 20, 1897, 1.
[18] *World,* Jan. 3, 1898, 1.
[19] 55 Congress, 2 Sess., *House Doc.* No. 409, 20, Lee, Consul-General at Havana to Day, Assistant Secretary of State, Jan. 18, 1898.
[20] *Idem.*

in turmoil.[21] One Spanish official was quoted as saying that the rioters should have gone further and have destroyed the offices "of that ——— paper, the New York *Journal*."[22] Newspaper correspondents in Havana stated that General Blanco, who had replaced Weyler, was powerless to control the situation and that American lives were in danger.[23] It was reported that deadly riots were hourly expected, and wild rumors came from Havana.[24] Meanwhile, the House was vigorously debating a resolution providing for recognition of Cuban belligerency which had already been approved by the Senate.[25]

Upon the request of Consul-General Lee, the battleship Maine was ordered to Havana on Jan. 24, 1898, on a "friendly visit."[26] Captain Sigsbee was in command of the vessel.[27] The *Journal* was elated over the sending of the Maine to Havana and in an editorial entitled, "Our Flag at Havana at Last," it said that "everything is now ready for the final scene, and it is to be hoped that it may not long be delayed."[28] It advocated that American vessels occupy all the Cuban ports at once with the demand that Spain withdraw her troops forthwith.[29] The New York *World* also felt that the day of Cuban deliverance was near.[30] Both newspapers announced that war was close at hand.[31]

Evidently the press was not alone in placing such an interpretation upon the turn of affairs, for such leaders as Senator Henry Cabot Lodge took a similar view of the situation. Writing to Henry White, Secretary to the American Embassy in London, Senator Lodge said:[32]

> There may be an explosion any day in Cuba which would settle a great many things. We have got a battleship in the harbor of Havana, and our fleet, which overmatches anything the Spaniards have, is masked at Dry Tortugas.

---

21 *World*, Jan. 14, 1898, 1.
22 *Journal*, Jan. 17, 1898, 1.
23 *World*, Jan. 17, 1898, 1.
24 *Ibid.*, Jan. 24, 1898, 1.
25 *Cong. Rec.*, 55 Congress, 2 Sess., XXXI, Pt. 1, 793-806, Jan. 20, 1898.
26 *House Doc.*, 405, 84, Lee to Day, Jan. 24, 1898.
27 *World*, Jan. 25, 1898, 1.
28 *Journal*, Jan. 26, 1898, 8.
29 *Ibid.*, Jan. 27, 1898, 8.
30 *World*, Jan. 25, 1898, 6.
31 *Cf. Journal, World*, Jan. 28, 1898, 1.
32 Allan Nevins, *Henry White; Thirty Years of American Diplomacy* (New York, 1930), 130.

It was during this tense period when public opinion in both countries was highly inflamed that the explosion of the Maine occurred on the night of Feb. 15, 1898.[33] The disaster was perhaps the biggest news event that had occurred since the assassination of President Garfield in 1881 and the sensational press "played up" the incident with all of the display at its command. Entire front pages were devoted to accounts of the explosion, and some newspapers gave over most of their editions to the catastrophe.[34]

Again the *Journal* and the *World* tried to outdo each other in the manner in which they handled the disaster. Additional correspondents were rushed to Havana in special tug boats or yachts accompanied by divers, who were expected to secure first-hand proof that the explosion was caused by a mine or torpedo. Naturally, these divers were not permitted to go near the wreckage.[35] Other New York papers were equally alert, if less aggressive, and the Associated Press carried complete reports of the explosion. For weeks after the disaster columns daily were written about the event.

Although the *World* and *Journal* had used striking headlines for months, the sinking of the Maine may be said to fix definitely the beginning of the practice on the part of most American newspapers of utilizing heavy type across several columns in displaying significant news, a practice which developed as the Spanish-American war progressed, leaving an indelible impress upon American journalism.

Both the *Journal* and the *World* published what they referred to as a "suppressed" cable message from Captain Sigsbee to Secretary of the Navy Long concerning the explosion of the vessel, which the reported "dispatches" asserted was not caused by an accident.[36] The New Orleans *Times-Democrat* charged that these reports were fabrications, as evidently they were.[37] There is no evidence to show that a "suppressed" cable message was dispatched to Long; certainly the Secretary of the Navy made no such sweeping assertions as were reported in the Pulitzer and Hearst papers. The *Journal* also asserted that United States divers,

[33] *House Doc.*, No. 405, 87, Lee to Day, Feb. 16, 1898.
[34] *Cf. World, Journal,* Boston *Herald,* Chicago *Tribune,* San Francisco *Chronicle,* Feb. 17, 1898.
[35] *World,* Feb. 19, 1898, 1.
[36] *Cf. Journal* and *World,* Feb. 17, 1898, 1.
[37] New Orleans *Times-Democrat,* Feb. 18, 1898, 4.

while seeking to find the bodies of the Maine victims, had uncovered evidence showing that the magazine had not been exploded and that "new proofs of treachery" had been found.[38] There seems to be no basis of fact for such an assertion. It was true that divers were employed in searching for bodies of victims, but no inspection of the wreckage was made until several weeks after the explosion when the Court of Inquiry began its investigation of the disaster. Even during the investigation made by the Court of Inquiry, which was conducted secretly, all information was carefully guarded from the press for obvious reasons.

The influence of the *Journal* in publishing "faked" news articles is clearly shown in the fact that the Associated Press carried news dispatches similar to the Hearst accounts concerning evidence uncovered by divers.[39] These reports were broadcast throughout the country and it seems reasonable to assume that thousands of Americans had definitely made up their minds that the explosion was the result of Spanish treachery long before an official investigation of the disaster was started.

Convinced that the Maine was deliberately blown up, the *Journal* set about to prove this contention, producing a sketch showing how the battleship was exploded by a mine or a torpedo, which was set off, it stated, by means of an electric current transmitted by wire from the shore.[40] It would seem that Hearst was determined to convince his readers that the disaster did not result from accident, and the *Journal* "artist" was instructed to produce a sketch conveying such an idea. The newspaper also used many illustrations of the Maine, its crew, and the way the vessel looked under water, most of which were products of the imagination of the *Journal* "artist." In addition, divers were pictured searching for the dead and "evidence that they were murdered under the murky waters of Havana Bay."[41] In view of the fact that divers at this time were searching for the dead, only a step was required in the imagination of readers to suppose that the former were also looking for evidence of Spain's guilt. The *Journal,* in its efforts to show that the disaster was caused by Spanish treachery, quoted numerous persons, in-

[38] *Journal,* Feb. 22, 1898, 6.
[39] *Times-Democrat,* Feb. 18, 1898, 4.
[40] *Journal,* Feb. 17, 1898, 1.
[41] *Ibid.,* Feb. 18, 1898, 4, 5.

cluding naval authorities, to the effect that the explosion was neither an accident nor had it come from within, as had been suggested.

Immediately following the explosion, the *Journal* offered a reward of $50,000 for the detection of the perpetrators of the deed and began to raise funds to build a national monument in memory of the Maine victims. In this connection it named a committee composed of prominent persons, which, the New York *Evening Post* contended, was done "to produce more credence for its lies and perversions."[42] The *Journal* sought to add the name of former President Cleveland to the committee but he refused to permit it, writing W. R. Hearst, publisher of the *Journal,* that he would not allow his sorrow "for those who died on the Maine to be perverted to an advertising scheme for the New York *Journal.*"[43] The *Journal,* in making the request, mentioned that Levi P. Morton, General Miles, Rear Admiral Selfridge, William C. Whitney, O. H. P. Belmont, George Gould, Chauncey M. Depew, Gen. O. O. Howard, the governors of fifteen states, the mayors of fifty-two cities, and a "large number of other citizens in public and private life" had accepted membership.

Announcing that the "*Journal's* patriotic cause is upheld by the pulpit," the Hearst paper said that one Brooklyn minister had used the newspaper's editorials as a text for his sermon.[44] In view of the *Journal's* tendency to exaggerate, the accuracy of this statement may be seriously questioned.

The *Journal* got out many "extra" editions, and a special train was employed to rush these to Washington.[45] "Banner" headlines were used frequently. At this time the *Journal* had two yachts, the "Anita" and the "Echo," and eight correspondents and "artists" in Havana, including Frederic Remington, James Creelman, Julian Hawthorne, Karl Decker, Alfred Henry Lewis, George Eugene Bryson, W. E. Lewis, and William Bengough.[46]

The *Journal* now started its "war scare" in earnest. Reporting that threats of war were coming from all over the country, it stated that the "whole country thrills with the

---

[42] *Cf.* New York *Evening Post,* March 28, 1898, 6.
[43] *Idem.*
[44] *Journal,* Feb. 21, 1898, 9.
[45] *Ibid.,* Feb. 17, 1898, 8.
[46] *Ibid.,* Feb. 24, 1898, 1.

war fever.'"[47] Brave Americans were ready to respond to the first call to arms, the newspaper said, and big monitors were being held in commission for an emergency.[48] Members of Congress were quoted as saying that intervention was an imperative duty; President McKinley was reported as arranging for a war loan; and the spirit of war throughout the country was gaining hourly in intensity, the *Journal* said, adding that citizens and soldiers were organizing and equipping for war. With a mighty army massing and ships ready to strike Havana, the United States, the *Journal* stated, was quite ready for the impending conflict.[49] And the next day, it announced that the "union is ablaze with patriotism" with every state ready to spring to arms at a moment's notice.[50] According to the *Journal,* Congress was prepared to force McKinley to act in the Cuban situation.[51] The *Journal's* aggressiveness resulted in its correspondents being barred from the Vizcaya, a Spanish vessel which had been dispatched to New York prior to the explosion of the Maine on a friendly visit, for fear they might attempt retaliatory measures.[52]

The pace set by the *Journal* was all but equaled by the *World* which had its special tug and correspondents with divers at Havana.[53] Using tactics similar to those employed by the *Journal,* the *World* quoted individuals as to their views on the explosion, and argued editorially that regardless of whether or not the disaster was caused by Spanish partisans or Cuban rebels, Spain was legally responsible for the deed.[54]

The *World* carried many news articles telling of preparations for war and the patriotic fervor "shown on all sides wherever people gather."[55] Every reference to the Maine or a war with Spain was enthusiastically received in theaters and other public places, the *World* stated, which it interpreted as evidence of "the warlike spirit of the multitude."[56] It went into detail in explaining how New York could be defended in case of war, with the final comment that the city

---

[47] *Ibid.*, Feb. 18, 1898, 1.
[48] *Ibid.*, 6.
[49] *Ibid.*, Feb. 24, 1898, 2.
[50] *Ibid.*, Feb. 25, 1898, 4, 5.
[51] *Ibid.*, Feb. 19, 1898, 8.
[52] *Ibid.*, Feb. 21, 1898, 1.
[53] *World*, Feb. 17, 1898, 1.
[54] *Ibid.*, Feb. 18, 1898, 6.
[55] *Ibid.*, Feb. 24, 1898, 3.
[56] *Ibid.*, Feb. 25, 1898, 3.

would be secure from attack.[57] Americans generally seemed to accept it as a fact, the *World* asserted, that the "Dons" were responsible for blowing up the Maine. According to the Pulitzer paper, the United States could raise an army of half a millon men in case of war,[58] and the House promised to vote $200,000,000 in case of an emergency for strengthening defenses.[59] It interviewed a large group of women in regard to the duty of "their menfolk,"[60] and gave the opinions of governors and newspaper editors concerning the disaster.[61]

Following the explosion, the *World* used daily a cartoon showing the horrors of the disaster.[62] Other illustrations were also carried, one of which portrayed Cuba shackled to Spain, and "Uncle Sam" in the act of drawing his sword, with the words, "The Only Atonement—Free Cuba."[63]

Other newspapers in every section of the country, particularly those securing news services from the New York papers, gave the news of the Maine disaster conspicuous display and commented editorially on the explosion. Following its usual policy in regard to the Cuban situation, the Boston *Herald* editorially took a conservative view of the situation while in its news columns it used reports of preparations for war with illustrations showing activities in the navy yards, which it received from the New York *Herald,* all of which were given prominent display.[64] In contrast to the *World* and *Journal,* the *Herald* emphasized editorially that the explosion of the Maine was accidental and that the public should withhold judgment until the facts were disclosed.[65] But during the latter part of February, the newspaper seemed to be led gradually to the conclusion that war was inevitable, and its news stories became more and more sensational as reports from New York of war preparations increased.[66]

Giving wide space to the Maine explosion and the news reports that followed, the New York *Sun* advocated quick action by Congress in the matter of strengthening coast defenses and adding to the small ships of the line.[67] The San

---

[57] *Ibid.,* Feb. 24, 1898, 2.
[58] *Ibid.,* 5.
[59] *Ibid.,* Feb. 25, 1898, 1.
[60] *Ibid.,* 4.
[61] *Ibid.,* Feb. 28, 1898, 4.
[62] *Cf. ibid.,* Feb. 18-28, 1898.
[63] *Ibid.,* Feb. 26, 1898, 5.
[64] *Cf. Herald,* Feb. 18-28, 1898.
[65] *Ibid.,* Feb. 17, 1898, 6.
[66] *Ibid.,* Feb. 20, 1898, 1; *ibid.,* Feb. 21, 1898, 1.
[67] New York *Sun,* Feb. 18, 1898, 1.

Francisco *Chronicle,* like the Boston *Herald,* pursued a news policy contradictory to its editorial policy. While asking through its editorials that the public suspend judgment until the Maine explosion was investigated, the *Chronicle* asserted, before any investigation had been made, that there was a strong suspicion that treachery was the cause of the catastrophe.[68] This inconsistency evidently resulted from the use of the New York *Herald* news service, which told of war preparations and "eloquent debates in the Senate for Cuban aid."[69] The *Times-Democrat* stated that war would be inevitable if it were shown that the explosion was caused by Spanish treachery.[70] With even reliable newspapers contending that the disaster was instigated by Spain, it is not surprising that the American public was convinced, long before the declaration of war, that a conflict would result.

Like the *Journal* and the *World,* the Chicago *Tribune* urged quick action on the part of Congress looking toward Cuban aid:[71]

> If the destruction of one of our most reliable battleships can arouse our national debating society to action—in place of words—the gain may be worth the sacrifice, though there is a sadly tragic side to it in the loss of over 250 lives of the nation's patriotic defenders.

The *Tribune* also told of war preparations and in one news report from Havana it stated that the Spaniards were "exulting over the Maine disaster."[72]

The Indianapolis *Journal* contended that "Spain should be driven off this hemisphere for the same reason that a community assumes the right to suppress a nuisance" and that "it must be evident to the most conservative and thoughtful men that the outcome of the present conditions is likely to be a collision with Spain."[73] The Indianapolis paper asserted that the chances of proving that the explosion was an accident were remote.[74] Both the Milwaukee *Sentinel* and the

---

68 San Francisco *Chronicle,* Feb. 17, 1898, 1, 2.
69 *Ibid.,* Feb. 18, 1898, 1; *ibid.,* Feb. 19, 1898, 3.
70 *Times-Democrat,* Feb. 19, 1898, 1.
71 Chicago *Tribune,* Feb. 17, 1898, 1.
72 *Ibid.,* Feb. 21, 1898, 1.
73 Indianapolis *Journal,* Feb. 25, 1898, 4; *ibid.,* March 1, 1898, 4.
74 *Ibid.,* Feb. 17, 1898, 6.

Washington *Post,* however, asked the public to withhold judgment until the matter had been investigated.[75]

The Maine explosion came at a time when public opinion in the United States and Spain had been inflamed by the press of both countries. The mystery surrounding the disaster and the rumors that arose as to the probable cause of the catastrophe presented opportunities for the sensational newspapers, which had been urging intervention of the United States in Cuba, to send out columns of dispatches, many of which were based upon nothing more tangible than mere speculation, which were distributed throughout the country. Immediately attributing the cause of the explosion to Spanish treachery, these newspapers gave a new impetus to the demand for intervention in Cuba and war with Spain.

[75] *Cf. Sentinel,* April 18, 1898, 1; *Post,* Feb. 17, 1898, 1.

CHAPTER VIII

THE DEMAND FOR WAR

Immediately following the Maine explosion a Court of Inquiry was appointed by the United States government to make an investigation of the disaster to determine its cause.[1] Its report, however, was not made public until late in March, approximately six weeks after the catastrophe.[2] During this period the partisan press continued to exploit the event, carrying news accounts daily of reported preparations for war and the expected findings of the Court of Inquiry, many of which were obviously based on rumor.[3] Thus, for weeks the Maine disaster was kept before the public.

Leading the other newspapers in the amount of news of the explosion, the preparations for war, and the illustrations it carried, the New York *Journal,* in striking manner, continued to urge Congress to take action to end Spanish rule in Cuba. *Journal* news stories told of the signing of contracts for guns; the activities of munitions factories and the navy yards;[4] and it proposed to raise a volunteer regiment on the Pacific coast for action in the conflict which it felt was approaching.[5] Despite McKinley's reiterated statement that the United States would take no action respecting the Maine disaster pending a report of the Court of Inquiry, the *Journal* pointed out the danger of delaying intervention in Cuba, asserting that Spain was borrowing millions and buying ships "to fight us while we quietly sit by awaiting developments."[6] According to a *Journal* dispatch, the Rothchilds had loaned Spain $40,000,000 at 40 per cent interest with which to buy warships which, it said, meant war "sure."[7] The next day the newspaper admitted that its dispatch was exaggerated, stating that Spain was only making a warlike pretense and that its reported loan was a "big sham."[8] The report in fact was not an exaggeration; it was clearly a misrepresentation

---

1 *World,* Feb. 17, 1898, 1.
2 *Journal,* March 29, 1898, 5.
3 *Cf. Journal, World, Sun,* New York *Herald,* Chicago *Tribune,* Boston *Herald,* San Francisco *Chronicle,* and Atlanta *Constitution,* Feb. 28, to March 29, 1898.
4 *Journal,* March 1, 1898, 1; *ibid.,* March 2, 1898, 2.
5 *Ibid.,* March 1, 1898, 5.
6 *Ibid.,* March 5, 1898, 1.
7 *Ibid.,* 2, 5.
8 *Ibid.,* March 6, 1898, 46.

without evidence to support it. Such "exaggerations," however, were not uncommon to the *Journal* at this time.

Reporting that Spain had demanded Consul-General Lee's recall, the *Journal* said that McKinley was convinced that Spain was about to declare war,[9] and later it announced in "banner" headlines that the United States was "nearer than ever to war with Spain" which, it said, was openly preparing for the conflict.[10] Spain's demand for Lee's recall was the occasion for an "extra" which was again rushed to Washington by the "*Journal* flyer."[11] Upon the introduction of a bill authorizing the President to spend $50,000,000 for the nation's defense, the *Journal,* in a "banner" headline announced: "For War! $50,000,000," adding that Democrats, Populists and Republicans, "in line with the *Journal's* advice," were backing the measure.[12]

The *Journal* published letters from individuals from different sections of the country declaring their willingness to fight,[13] and it quoted Theodore Roosevelt as saying that "we should wipe the Spanish flag from the seas."[14] It also published a purported interview with Roosevelt in which he was reported as stating that "the *Journal's* Washington war news is correct."[15] Roosevelt vehemently denied having given the interview.[16]

Adding a "Summary of the Latest War News" to its innovations, the newspaper reported that the Triple Alliance, composed of Germany, Austria-Hungary, and Italy, would back Spain in demanding an international court to settle the Maine issue,[17] but this proposal was rejected by the United States "with scorn," the *Journal* said, adding that the crisis of war or peace depended upon whether or not the Spanish flotilla started westward from the Canary Islands.[18] When the Spanish fleet moved westward, the newspaper announced that the United States had ordered final preparations for a conflict and that "the roll of the stirring drum and the trum-

---

[9] *Ibid.*, 47.
[10] *Ibid.*, March 7, 1898, 1.
[11] *Ibid.*, 5.
[12] *Ibid.*, March 8, 1898, 1.
[13] *Ibid.*, March 14, 1898, 6.
[14] *Ibid.*, March 15, 1898, 1.
[15] *Ibid.*, March 19, 1898, 1.
[16] *Ibid.*, March 23, 1898, 6. Roosevelt in later years frequently denied statements attributed to him by reputable journalists which tendency gave rise to the feeling among some newspapermen that he was not above reproach in this respect.
[17] *Ibid.*, March 18, 1898, 2.
[18] *Ibid.*, March 19, 1898, 1.

pet sings of fame.'"[19] The Hearst paper urged the United States to intercept the fleet before it reached the West Indies.[20] During this period Cuban partisans in Congress were making vigorous speeches in favor of the rebels.[21]

President E. Benjamin Andrews of Brown University was quoted by the *Journal* as saying that "war is a good medicine,"[22] and Dr. Lyman Abbott was reported as asserting in a sermon in Brooklyn that he favored freeing Cuba.[23]

Secretary Long was quoted as saying, after a cabinet meeting, that the "elements of Spanish official responsibility for the Maine explosion might be considered eliminated," following which the Hearst paper charged that the Secretary and Mark Hanna had betrayed the nation to "Wall Street."[24] The *Journal* stated that Hanna had advised his friends prior to the announcement to buy stocks, which, after the cabinet meeting and the Secretary's reported statement, advanced several points netting them $20,000,000.[25] McKinley was also accused of being influenced by financial interests.[26]

A "Congressional Commission," composed of Senators Thurston of Nebraska, Money of Mississippi, and Gallinger of New Hampshire, and Representatives Cummings of New York and William Alden Smith of Michigan, was sent to Cuba early in March by the *Journal* aboard its yacht, "Anita," to secure first-hand information concerning conditions on the island.[27] Cummings was a member of the House Committee on Naval Affairs and Smith, a member of the Foreign Affairs Committee. Referring to the group as "commissioners" and "envoys," the *Journal* said that the "brave congressmen faced death to get at the truth in Cuba."[28] Each member of the party contributed articles to the *Journal* describing the suffering and privations of the people on the island.[29] Mrs. Thurston, who had accompanied the Nebraska Senator on the journey, wrote an appeal to the mothers of the United States:[30]

---

[19] *Ibid.*, March 25, 1898, 1, 2.
[20] *Ibid.*, 6.
[21] *Ibid.*, March 18, 1898, 3.
[22] *Ibid.*, March 4, 1898, 5.
[23] *Ibid.*, March 14, 1898, 1.
[24] *Ibid.*, March 4, 1898, 3.
[25] *Idem.*
[26] *Ibid.*, April 8, 1898, 3.
[27] *Ibid.*, March 2, 1898, 1. Money had been elected to the Senate to fill the unexpired term of Senator J. Z. George, who had died in office.
[28] *Ibid.*, March 6, 1898, 49.
[29] *Ibid.*, March 14, 1898, 6.
[30] *Ibid.*, March 13, 1898, 41.

> Oh! Mothers of the Northland, who tenderly clasp your little ones to your loving hearts! Think of the black despair that filled each mother's heart as she felt her life-blood ebb away, and knew that she had left her little ones to perish from the pain of starvation and disease.

Mrs. Thurston died while on the island, "pitying Cuba."[31]

Following the inspection trip to Cuba, the "commissioners" reported conditions on the island in speeches before Congress, asserting that the newspaper accounts were not exaggerated and that the *Journal* was inspired by patriotic motives in striving to aid the rebels.[32] McKinley was reported as saying that the "commissioners' report could not fail to be of great value."[33] The New York *Evening Post,* however, was not so complimentary in its remarks concerning the value of the report:[34]

> Nevertheless when one of them (yellow journals) offers a yacht voyage, with free wine, rum and cigars, and a good bed, under the guise of philanthropy, or gets up a committee for Holy purposes, and promises to puff it, it can get almost any one it pleases to go on the yacht voyage and serve on the committee—senators, lawyers, divines, scholars, poets, presidents and what not.

After interviewing members of Congress, the *Journal* announced that Congress was ready and eager to fight, and in the same issue it carried a cartoon showing "Uncle Sam" shackled in stocks and being tormented by a "Spanish Don."[35] The newspaper reported that McKinley's program included "the Maine report, message to Congress, and immediate intervention in Cuba."[36] When the President dispatched a note to Spain asking that she grant Cuban independence, the *Journal* again interviewed senators and representatives as to what action they thought the United States should take in the event Spain refused the request of the President.[37] The

---

31 *Ibid.,* March 16, 1898, 2.
32 *Ibid.,* March 25, 1898, 5.
33 *Ibid.,* March 24, 1898, 1.
34 *Evening Post,* March 17, 1898, 6.
35 *Journal,* March 29, 1898, 1.
36 *Ibid.,* March 23, 1898, 1.
37 *Ibid.,* April 1, 1898, 2.

members of Congress, according to the *Journal,* replied that such refusal would be grounds for war.

Long before the Court of Inquiry had made its report, the *Journal* announced that the court's verdict was that "Spain is guilty."[38] It also stated that the report of the Court of Inquiry showed that the plates from the keel of the Maine to the water's edge at the deck had been pushed up, proving that the explosion had come from the outside and not from the inside as had been suggested by the Spanish Board of Inquiry, which was also at work on the case.[39] On the following day, the *Journal* announced that the "Court of Inquiry finds that Spanish government officials blew up the Maine" and that the "cruiser was purposely moved where a Spanish mine exploded by Spanish officers would destroy it."[40] It then decided that "Weyler's mine destroyed the Maine" after the former Captain-General had written a letter to a Spanish newspaper in which he discussed the disaster.[41] With the headline, "Abstract of the Court of Inquiry Report Shows the Maine Was Blown Up Exactly as the *Journal* Described It," the newspaper, while admitting that the official report had not been sent to Washington, asserted that an abstract of the report had reached the capital.[42] The news story used under the headline, however, merely stated that the abstract "is said to verify the forecast published in the *Journal* on March 10." Reiterating that the report of the Court of Inquiry showed that the battleship was blown up by a mine or torpedo, the Hearst paper announced that "actual declaration of war with Spain now seems to be only a few days away."[43] It also stated that the testimony given before the court, the sessions of which were conducted secretly, was "too strong for publication."[44] Considering that the testimony was unavailable, this sensational statement served as an effective substitute for the news report that the *Journal* evidently desired.

When the court finally completed its hearings and the report was sent to Washington precautions were taken to prevent its being intercepted and published prematurely by

---

[38] *Ibid.,* April 4, 1898, 1.
[39] *Ibid.,* March 10, 1898, 1.
[40] *Ibid.,* March 11, 1898, 1
[41] *Ibid.,* March 18, 1898, 5.
[42] *Ibid.,* March 20, 1898, 1.
[43] *Ibid.,* March 26, 1898, 1.
[44] *Ibid.,* March 28, 1898, 1.

the newspapers.[45] The official report of the court was to the effect that the Maine was destroyed by the explosion of a submarine mine which caused the partial explosion of two or more of her forward magazines.[46] The court did not fix responsibility. The *Journal,* however, stated that "suppressed testimony shows Spain is guilty of blowing up the Maine."[47]

Negotiations between Spain and the United States were opened following the report of the Court of Inquiry to settle the controversy arising from the Maine disaster, but the former, refusing to discuss the question of Cuban freedom which had been projected by this country, broke off the negotiations.[48] The *Journal* now predicted that McKinley would send a message to Congress urging intervention and when he failed to do so, the newspaper said that the President had "deliberately tricked Congress and the people."[49] The Hearst paper stated that "it is now up to Congress" to act since the President had refused to recommend intervention.[50]

The Journal "played up" the accounts of the burial of the Maine victims with numerous illustrations.[51] It also published a letter from a mother of a Maine victim with the headline: "American Mother of Maine Victim Appeals to the Nation for Revenge."[52]

The news and editorial policy of the *World* during the period between the Maine explosion and the declaration of war was quite similar to that of the *Journal.* The *World* published purported quotations of members of Congress to the effect that money indemnity would not satisfy the people of the United States.[53] Writing to the *World* from Havana, Scovel asserted that a "Spanish general on the very day that the Maine was destroyed" had remarked: "We are going to blow her up mighty soon."[54] Shortly thereafter the Pulitzer paper announced that "final and clinching proof" had been uncovered proving that the Maine was blown up by design, by mine or torpedo, but it did not explain what

---

45 New York *Evening Post,* March 21, 1898, 1.
46 *Journal,* March 29, 1898, 5.
47 *Ibid.,* April 2, 1898, 1.
48 *Ibid.,* April 4, 1898, 1.
49 *Ibid.,* April 7, 1898, 1.
50 *Ibid.,* April 9, 1898, 3.
51 *Ibid.,* March 12, 1898, 3.
52 *Ibid.,* April 9, 1898, 1.
53 *World,* March 1, 1898, 6.
54 *Ibid.,* March 2, 1898, 6.

the final proof was nor by whom it had been uncovered.[55] Other news stories tended to show that a plot to blow up the Maine was known. One of these told about an "elderly Spaniard who implored the American consulate to 'send the Maine away! For God's sake send the Maine away!' "[56] What ever Spain's connection with the Maine disaster was, the *World* said, the duty of the United States "to put her off the continent is clear and plain."[57] After quoting Secretary of the Treasury Gage to the effect that war would be "declared in fifteen minutes if it is proved that the Maine explosion was caused by the Spaniards," the newspaper pointed out that certain facts had already been established by the *World* tending to show that Spanish treachery was responsible for the explosion.[58]

The Pulitzer paper was clearly disappointed over the failure of the Court of Inquiry to fix responsibility;[59] it asserted, however, that the evidence taken by the court indicated that the explosion was caused by a floating submarine mine; and it concluded that the "Spaniards planted the mine and had exact knowledge of its whereabouts; they had the Maine anchored over it; they controlled its connections; and they are accountable for its explosion, whether cognizant or not of the hand that pressed the button."[60] It added that "the government of Spain is inescapably responsible for the destruction of the Maine by a MINE in Havana harbor."[61] "What are we going to do about it?" it asked.

Commenting editorially on the responsibility for the disaster, the *World* said:[62]

> Regardless of the question of Cuban independence, unless it be the crowning reason for interference, the destruction of the Maine by foul play should be the occasion of ordering our fleet to Havana and demanding proper amends within forty-eight hours under threat of bombardment. If Spain will not punish her miscreants, we must punish Spain.

---

55 *Ibid.*, March 12, 1898, 1.
56 *Ibid.*, March 3, 1898, 6.
57 *Ibid.*, March 2, 1898, 6.
58 *Ibid.*, March 20, 1898, 1, 4-6.
59 *Ibid.*, March 26, 1898, 1.
60 *Ibid.*, March 29, 1898, 6.
61 *Ibid.*, March 31, 1898, 6.
62 *Ibid.*, April 1, 1898, 6.

> In brief, the Maine was deliberately destroyed by means carefully prepared in advance which means were under absolute control of the Spanish authorities.
>
> Spain's responsibility is complete. Yet, as the ambassador has said, "Spain has stood mute and like a wolf takes the consequences of the villainy of her cub!"
>
> But was it the cub?

Again the Pulitzer paper asserted that the explosion of the Maine "was an act of war," asking, "Are we waiting to be smitten on the other cheek?"[63]

The *World* published an article written by J. P. Gibbons, purportedly an English expert under whose patents mines were made for Spain, in which it was stated that the mine which blew up the Maine "was deliberately set off;" that the statements of the Spanish legation at Washington and of Weyler that there were no submarine mines in Havana harbor were not correct as he (Gibbons) had shipped mines for Havana on a Spanish ship, the property of the Spanish government, and commanded by Spanish naval officers.[64] The author of the article was quoted as saying that his mines were in electrical connection with the shore, and that it was impossible that they could be exploded except by design.

The *World* used pictures of the maimed victims of the Maine disaster and many cartoons, one of which showed "Uncle Sam" without coat and hat rolling up his sleeves with his eyes on devastated Cuba and the caption: "Peace, by Jingo, If I Have to Fight For It."[65] Beginning with the announcement of the explosion, the newspaper ran daily at the head of its editorial column the statement: "They died that Cuba might be free;" and later it gave daily the total number of days since the disaster with a criticism of the administration for its alleged inactivity in not demanding satisfaction.[66] Referring to the 266 officers and seamen who had lost their lives in the explosion, the *World* asked:[67]

> Will this be the epitaph for these brave soldiers of ours: "They died that Cuba might be free!"

In a series of editorials entitled, "Peace—with a But," the *World* argued that the people wanted peace but "Cuba must

[63] *Ibid.*, April 5, 1898, 6.
[64] *Ibid.*, April 8, 1898, 1.
[65] *Ibid.*, March 4, 1898, 7.
[66] *Ibid.*, April 2, 1898, 6.
[67] *Ibid.*, March 10, 1898, 6.

be free.'"[68] In one issue it ran ten editorials on the Cuban question, all of which were concluded with demands for immediate action on the part of the United States.[69]

While it was attempting to show that the Maine explosion was caused by Spanish treachery, the *World*, like the *Journal*, carried news articles telling of preparations for war. It queried members of Congress and governors of states for expressions of opinions as to the duty of the nation in the crisis, and these declared, according to the *World*, that if an official investigation disclosed Spanish treachery they would back the President in any demand he might make on Spain "to include large indemnity and the freedom of Cuba and if these are refused, war must be declared.'"[70] Announcing that Secretary of War Alger, Secretary Sherman, and Joseph W. Bailey of Texas, Democratic leader in the House of Representatives, in messages to the *World*, had emphasized the danger of war, the newspaper said that McKinley "is now ready for war" and that all "Europe regards war as now certain.'"[71] When the House without a dissenting vote passed the measure appropriating $50,000,000 for defense, the *World* stated that Congress as one man had said that "we don't war, but if it must come let it come now—we are ready.'"[72] A few days later, with a "banner" headline the Pulitzer paper announced that "We Are Ready.'"[73] It quoted Rep. Richard P. Bland of Missouri as saying that unless the administration drove the Spaniards out of Cuba "the people of this country are going to ask the reason why, and their demands will be strong and emphatic.'"[74]

The first three pages of every issue of the *World*, from the time of the explosion until the declaration of war, were devoted to Cuban news, principally accounts telling of plans for war. Senators Hale of Maine, Mills of Texas, and Morgan of Alabama were quoted to the effect that the United States must intervene in Cuba even if war should result.[75] Continuing its accounts of war preparations, the *World*, after reporting that the Spanish flotilla had sailed from the

[68] *Ibid.*, March 5, 1898, 6.
[69] *Ibid.*, April 6, 1898, 6.
[70] *Ibid.*, March 6, 1898, 4.
[71] *Ibid.*, March 8, 1898, 1.
[72] *Ibid.*, March 9, 1898, 1.
[73] *Ibid.*, March 13, 1898, 1.
[74] *Ibid.*, March 19, 1898, 2.
[75] *Ibid.*, March 22, 1898, 1; *ibid.*, March 23, 1898, 1-3.

Canary Islands for Porto Rico, announced that the United States could land 80,000 troops in Cuba within ten days.[76] The *World* was convinced that if war came it would not last long.

When McKinley refused to take decisive action, following the breaking off of negotiations with Spain, the Pulitzer paper said that Congress was in open revolt and that Cuban freedom was near.[77] In one day, eight resolutions were introduced in Congress, two declaring war against Spain, three calling for forcible intervention to end the Cuban conflict, and three recognizing the independence of the island.[78] Following the introduction of these measures, the *World* announced that McKinley had given Spain forty-eight hours in which to decide whether or not she would grant Cuban independence,[79] after which it asserted that "no one knows what today may bring forth—nothing now is certain except that war is imminent."[80] In New York a bill appropriating $1,000,000 for defraying the expenses of the national guard and naval militia of the state in a war with Spain, the *World* reported, was passed by the legislature and signed by the governor within ninety minutes.[81] After telling about activities of the American fleet at Key West, the newspaper, with a "banner" headline, announced that a "Great Battle May Be Fought Within Five Days," and in the same issue it stated that there would be "from two to five days more for a polite exchange of formal notes between the United States and Spain—and then war."[82] But it would not be "much of a war."[83]

The *World* conducted a poll of every congressional district in every state in the union, questioning "representative men of every occupation" as to their views on the Cuban question, and with a headline across two pages, it announced that the sentiment of the nation on the Cuban issue was that there should be "No More Delay."[84] On the following day, it stated that the President and Congress were united for war, adding that Spain had been given five days of grace "before an ultimatum will be sent by the United States" after which hostilities would begin if she did not agree to

[76] *Ibid.*, March 24, 1898, 3.
[77] *Ibid.*, March 30, 1898, 1.
[78] *Ibid.*, 2.
[79] *Ibid.*, March 31, 1898, 1.
[80] *Ibid.*, April 1, 1898, 1.
[81] *Ibid.*, 2.
[82] *Ibid.*, April 2, 1898, 1.
[83] *Ibid.*, 6.
[84] *Ibid.*, April 6, 1898, 4-5.

give up Cuba.[85] When the *World's* prediction failed to materialize, it became impatient at the delay, commenting editorially:[86]

> Parley, parley, parley! Delay, delay, delay! "To-morrow" is the motto of Spain!
>
> Stop the nonsense! Let us have peace even if we must fight a battle or two to compel it!

At this time Joseph Pulitzer, editor and publisher of the *World,* was personally directing the editorial policy of the paper and writing some of the editorials.[87]

The extent and growth in circulation of the *Journal* and the *World* during the early part of 1898 is difficult to determine accurately because of the lack of authentic records.[88] However, if the circulation figures as announced by the two papers can be accepted as approximating the increase in circulation, the growth of both publications must have been rapid. In March, 1897, the *Journal* announced that the combined circulation of its morning and evening papers was 750,000.[89] The *Sunday Journal* carried 104 pages on Dec. 5, 1897,[90] and a few days later the newspaper asserted that its Sunday edition was read by 2,500,000.[91] The Hearst paper stated in April, 1898, that the combined circulation of its morning and evening papers totaled 1,000,000, an increase of 250,000 over the combined circulation at approximately the same time of the previous year.[92]

The *World* boasted that the combined circulation of its morning and evening papers for the month of March, 1898, averaged 822,804 daily, a gain over March, 1897, of 109,486.[93]

Other newspapers, especially those using the news services of New York papers, followed in a less aggressive way the lead of the *Journal* and *World* in "playing up" the Maine explosion and war preparations. The Boston *Herald,* in a news story sent out by the New York *Herald,* announced before the Court of Inquiry had given its findings, that dis-

[85] *Ibid.,* April 7, 1898, 1.
[86] *Ibid.,* April 11, 1898, 6.
[87] *Cf. ibid.,* April 10, 1898, 6. Several of the editorials during this period were signed with the name of Joseph Pulitzer.
[88] Probably the best available record of newspaper circulation for this period is N. W. Ayer & Son's *American Newspaper Annual,* but since the reports contained therein are based largely on publishers' statements the figures can hardly be accepted at their face value.
[89] *Journal,* March 24, 1897, 2.
[90] *Cf. ibid.,* Dec. 5, 1897.
[91] *Ibid.,* Dec. 9, 1897, 8.
[92] *Ibid.,* April 4, 1898, 6.
[93] *World,* April 3, 1898, 6.

coveries made by divers indicated that the Maine was not destroyed by accident.[94] This report was in effect the same as that published by the *Journal* and, like the latter's dispatch, was manifestly inaccurate. The *Herald* also carried news stories telling of preparations for war.[95] In brief, the New York *Herald* service was quite as unreliable and exaggerated, if less sensational, as that of the *World* or *Journal.*

The San Francisco *Chronicle,* which was using the *Sun* service at this time, "played up" news accounts of preparations for war, and stated that "if war comes we shall be prepared."[96] The *Sun* service was likewise of a sensational nature.

Using a special news service, the Indianapolis *Journal* also published stories dealing with war plans and emphasizing the war hysteria in this country;[97] and the New Orleans *Times-Democrat* published excerpts, announcing preparations for war, from the *World,* the New York *Herald,* the *Sun,* and the Chicago *Tribune,* in addition to Associated Press dispatches.[98]

The Chicago *Tribune* at this time was using both the *World* and *Journal* services and carried the most striking news articles from each paper, while the Atlanta *Constitution,* which also received a special news service, published accounts to the effect that war was inevitable.[99] The latter carried the account of the "suppressed" dispatch from Captain Sigsbee to Secretary Long stating that the Maine explosion was not caused by an accident.[100] This fact would indicate that it was using the *Journal* service. With the headline, "Divers Disclose the Deed of a Dastard, the Hand of a Spaniard Did the Work," the *Constitution* gave prominent display to reports of the cause of the disaster before the Court of Inquiry was well started in its investigation.[101] It also interviewed several hundred persons in Atlanta to determine their views on the cause of the explosion, after which it announced that, "Ninety Per Cent of the People of Atlanta Believe the Maine was Wrecked by Treachery."[102]

---

[94] Boston *Herald,* Feb. 23, 1898, 1.
[95] *Ibid.,* Feb. 22, 1898, 1.
[96] *Chronicle,* Feb. 22, 1898, 1.
[97] *Journal,* Feb. 26, 1898, 1.
[98] *Times-Democrat,* Feb. 22, 1898, 7.
[99] Atlanta *Constitution,* Feb. 21, 1898, 1.
[100] *Ibid.,* Feb. 23, 1898, 1.
[101] *Ibid.,* Feb. 24, 1898, 1.
[102] *Ibid.,* Feb. 17, 1898, 1.

This broad generalization indicates the sensational manner in which its news from Cuba was handled.

After months of persistent campaigning for intervention in Cuba, the partisan press greeted with an outward show of exultation the announcement that President McKinley, in his message to Congress on April 11, had asked for authority to intervene in the island. The House was not slow in taking action and on April 13, by a vote of 322 to 19, it adopted a resolution directing the President to intervene at once to stop the war in Cuba.[103] Three days later the Senate, by a vote of 67 to 21, approved the Foraker resolution declaring that the government of the United States recognized the Republic of Cuba, after an amendment offered by Senator Teller of Colorado disclaiming annexation had been adopted and the house resolution had been rejected.[104] The two houses finally reached an agreement on a resolution, April 18, when the Senate receded from its original position and agreed to the House measure which did not recognize the Cuban Republic but merely authorized the President to use the land and naval forces of the United States to end the war in Cuba.[105] Diplomatic relations with Spain were severed on April 21, but it was not until April 24 that a bill was passed by Congress declaring that war existed between the United States and Spain and had existed since April 21.[106]

[103] New York *Journal*, April 14, 1898, 1.
[104] Boston *Herald*, April 17, 1898, 1.
[105] *Ibid.*, April 19, 1898, 1.
[106] *World*, April 25, 1898, 1.

CHAPTER IX

MISREPRESENTATIONS OF THE "YELLOW PRESS"

The Maine disaster may be said to have been the immediate cause of the war with Spain. For approximately three years sensational newspapers in this country had campaigned vigorously for the cause of the rebels, but prior to the Maine explosion their news, though arousing sympathy for the Cubans, was lacking in those elements necessary to crystallize American sentiment in favor of war with Spain. These newspapers had made the most of the incidents growing out of filibustering and had persistently urged the United States to recognize Cuban belligerency. Following the lead of the *World,* they had exploited Spanish "atrocities" on the island, and the New York *Journal,* impatient at the way events were moving, had resorted to an aggressive policy in uncovering several episodes that stirred the country. For some time a large part of the American public had indicated their opposition to Spain, but the spark needed to explode their pent-up feelings against Spanish "oppression" had failed to materialize. This spark was furnished in the Maine disaster.

The Maine disaster also was the occasion for sensational newspapers to recapitulate their demands for a cessation of the rebellion in Cuba and for Cuban independence. The mystery surrounding the catastrophe, which sent 266 officers and seamen to their death, and the suspicion of Spanish treachery furnished the basis for many rumors and speculations as to the cause of the explosion, which were used to advantage by several newspapers, especially the *World* and *Journal,* in inflaming the minds of the people.[1]

That many of the news reports concerning the disaster and the subsequent developments were based on rumors or "faked" has been shown frequently. The *Journal* and the *World* particularly were guilty of misrepresentations. Spain's "money loan" from the Rothchilds to buy warships was admittedly false. The *Journal's* "commission" was, as E. L. Godkin's paper asserted, primarily a scheme for self aggrandizement. The Hearst paper probably experienced little

[1] Chicago *Times-Herald,* Feb. 19, 1898, 2.

difficulty in persuading members of Congress to make the journey which, with all expenses paid, was in the nature of a pleasure trip. Could any member of the "commission" do other than "puff" the *Journal* upon his return? Without the co-operation of "jingo" senators and representatives, newspaper propaganda for the Cubans would have proved less effective.

The manner in which both the Hearst and the Pulitzer papers handled reports of the sessions of the Court of Inquiry further indicates the biased policies of these papers. The proceedings were unavailable for publication because the sessions were secret. But this fact did not deter the resourceful correspondents, and "news" stories based on rumors and at times apparently on imagination were dispatched regularly. Reports of "suppressed" testimony taken before the court and the "suppressed" dispatch were more effective perhaps in obtaining reaction on the part of readers than accurate accounts would have been. The effect of exaggerated reports in the *World* and *Journal* also led other papers to use similar accounts; thus inaccurate news articles were broadcast. The *Journal's* "War News Summary," which might have been intended to apply to the Cuban conflict but which to many readers meant the prospective war between this country and Spain, is another example of clever misrepresentation.

The practice of conducting polls of members of Congress, governors and other public officials to determine their views on the Cuban question was an insidious means of spreading propaganda. In this way newspapers were enabled to make exaggerated claims which could not be substantiated by the results of such polls. The *World's* poll of every congressional district in the country was reported as showing the sense of the people on the Cuban situation; actually the number replying to the questionnaire was entirely too small to represent American opinion. Then, too, it is possible that only those who felt strongly on the matter replied in which case the poll indicated nothing.

The use of shrieking headlines, which frequently misrepresented already exaggerated news dispatches, was one of the most pernicious practices employed by "yellow journals." Rational readers undoubtedly discounted much of what these sensational papers published, but there were many who evidently were incapable of properly interpreting the events to whom such misleading reports meant but one thing—that this country was on the brink of war.

Further evidence that many of the news reports concerning the Maine disaster were misleading is shown by the severe criticisms made against "yellow journals" by responsible newspapers of that period and by later authors. Particularly caustic in their criticism of "yellow journals" were the New York *Evening Post* and *The Nation,* of which E. L. Godkin was editor. In discussing the practices of sensational papers following the Maine explosion, *The Nation* commented:[2]

> . . . Certainly if ever the ministry feels itself called upon to withstand the active powers of darkness, the need of opposing and exposing the diabolical newspapers which are trying to lie the country into war must be obvious. The trouble is that the lying is so devilish that it perverts even words of truth and soberness that any sane and honest man may speak. It seems impossible to give the lie to these venal and unspeakable sheets in so explicit endorsement. Luckily the lying has been done on such a monstrous scale that nothing these papers say is now credited by any rational man without independent confirmation. A long course of lies, which, like the father that begets them are gross as a mountain, open, palpable, is at last working out the natural result of breeding universal distrust of anything seen in print. But the liars go jauntily on to the lake of fire prepared for them.
>
> Nothing could be more curious than the contrast between the wild aspect of the first pages of our penny dreadfuls and the calm demeanor of the persons who are seen reading them. If half of what the "scare" headlines reveal were true, the first impulse of the reader would be to remove his family to a place of safety, dispose of his property as best he could, and make arrangements to leave the country. A few years ago the mere sight of a newspaper got up in this extraordinary style, with headlines in bill poster type reaching quite across the page, would have started a

[2] *The Nation,* LXVI, March 3, 1898, 157.

panic. People would have inferred that nothing less than a most dangerous condition of affairs could have led the editor to such unusual demonstrations of alarm. Now they are read with entire passivity, even although they declare war to be imminent, and indicate that a majority of the American people including those of them who are in power, are either lunatics or maniacs. The new journalism has been steadily raising the tone of its yelling till it has reached the highest limit possible. The louder it shrieks, the less attention is paid to it. What would remain for it to do in case of real danger, or a real war, it is difficult to imagine. The resources of type have been exhausted. Nothing in the way of larger letters can be used, unless only a single headline is to be given on the first page. Red ink has been resorted to as an additional element of attraction or terror, and if we had a war, the whole paper might be printed in red, white, and blue. In that case, real instead of imitation lunatics should be employed as editors, and contributors.

Continuing its criticism in a lead editorial in the following issue, *The Nation* said:[3]

. . . The 3,000 miles distance that lies between us and Spain muffles the defiance hurled by our yellow journals and the answering ones of the *Globo,* the *Correo,* and the *Imparcial* of Madrid, leaving them free to "scoop" each other and the public without much harm. One of these yellow journals says that its Madrid dispatch of Thursday was stopped by the censorship—for good reasons, no doubt. . . .

Our usually cool contemporary, the Chicago *Tribune,* follows up its article declaring that "war exists" with one showing why it ought to exist, the inference being that it exists figuratively, only, at the present time. A figurative war is cheaper than an actual one, and therefore to be preferred on some accounts. The *Tribune's* reasons why war ought to exist are of a varied character, implying great penetration on the part of their discoverer into the deeper springs of human action. One of these is that "it (war)

[3] *Ibid.,* LXVI, March 10, 1898, 175.

would wipe out mugwumpery, which is trying to choke out the vigorous life of the nation." This is said to be one of the desirable consequences of a war with Spain. But why not a war with England, or Japan, or Turkey, or Chili, or Germany? Is there anything about a war with Spain that should make it peculiarly destructive to mugwumpery? As for war in the abstract, if we can imagine such a thing, its most pronounced advocate hitherto has been the Hon. Theodore Roosevelt, who is also, in the opinion of many Republicans of the Empire State, strongly tinged with mugwumpery. Indeed, the Chicago *Tribune* has been under suspicions of the same sort. Now, we object strongly to wiping out mugwumps by means of a war with Spain.

Referring to the influence of newspapers on diplomatic negotiations, Godkin asserted elsewhere that newspapers frequently advocated war because "they have to maintain their place in the estimation of their readers, and, if possible, to increase the number of these readers."[4] Continuing his discussion, Godkin said:[5]

> Newspapers are made to sell; and for this purpose there is nothing better than war. War means daily sensation and excitement. On this almost any kind of newspaper may live and make money. Whether the war brings victory or defeat makes little difference. The important thing is that in war every moment may bring important and exciting news,—news which does not need to be accurate or to bear sifting. What makes it most marketable is that it is probable and agreeable, although disagreeable news sells nearly as well. . . .
>
> It follows from this, it cannot but follow, that it is only human for a newspaper proprietor to desire war, especially when he feels sure that his own country is right, and that its opponents are enemies of civilization,—a state of mind into which a man may easily work himself by writing and talking much during an

[4] E. L. Godkin, "The Growth and Expansion of Public Opinion" in *The Atlantic Monthly*, LXXXI, January, 1898, 9.
[5] *Idem.*

> international controversy. So that I do not think it an exaggeration or a calumny to say that the press, taken as a whole,—of course with many honorable exceptions,—has a bias in favor of war. It would stir up a war with any country, but if it sees preparations made to fight, it does not fail to encourage the combatants.

Discussing the practices of sensational journals, the *Evening Post* asserted:[6]

> Every one who knows anything about "yellow journals" knows that everything they do and say is intended to promote sales, or, in other words, is meant to be an advertisement of the paper and show the power of "Journalism." Therefore they are always trying to do something queer and big, so as to attract more attention and sell more copies. Predictions of war and reasons why war is inevitable are of the same mental and moral value as puffs of shoes or of quack medicines. Insofar, therefore, as these papers are public evils, and a national disgrace to be got rid of if possible, the best service any man can render to the state is to refuse to aid and abet them in any schemes for attracting notice to themselves. Yet how few men, however highly placed, there seem to be who are capable of this trifling act of patriotism. No one—absolutely no one—supposes a yellow journal cares five cents about the Cubans, the Maine victims, or any one else. A yellow journal is probably the nearest approach to hell, existing in any Christian state.

Later, the *Evening Post* remarked:[7]

> During the present war crisis, their lying with the view of promoting the outbreak of a war, has excited the disgust and reprobation of all the intelligent portion of the nation.

Referring to the purported Roosevelt interview published in the New York *Journal*, the *Evening Post* said that the Assistant Secretary of the Navy had written a letter to "a yellow journal which had invented an interview with him, a

[6] New York *Evening Post*, March 17, 1898, 6.
[7] *Ibid.*, March 28, 1898, 6.

frequent yellow practice.'"[8] Roosevelt was quoted by the *Evening Post* as saying that the statement published in the New York *Journal* was an "absolute falsehood.'"[9]

In attempting to show that the "yellow journals" were not interested in the welfare of the Cubans as they contended they were, Godkin's paper referred to the Kansas City *Star,* which sent its Washington correspondent, Albert Miller, to Cuba to observe and report on conditions there.[10] Instead of trying to inflame the public mind with gross exaggerations, the *Evening Post* explained, or with articles woven out of "purely imaginative material," the correspondent looked for the worst suffering in Cuba, found it, and returned to this country to obtain aid.[11] This example showed, it was contended, "the thoroughly practical form which American sympathy can take, as distinguished from mere newspaper booms and hippodrome journalism.'"[12]

The Nation asserted that many of the "news" reports of evidence being uncovered following the Maine disaster were nothing more than "fakes.'"[13] Discussing false newspaper reports concerning the explosion, *The Nation* referred to a news report to the effect that 2,000 Americans in Havana would be in danger if the President sent his message to Congress before giving the Consul-General time to get them out.[14] It was later shown that there were only 200 Americans in Cuba at that time.[15]

Both the Indianapolis *Journal* and the San Francisco *Chronicle* held up to ridicule the "faking" of "yellow journals," particularly with reference to their stories of the Maine disaster,[16] and the Milwaukee *Sentinel* criticized the New York *World,* the New York *Journal,* Chicago *Tribune,* and the Chicago *Times-Herald* for their alleged practice of "yellow journalism:'"[17]

> Is it too much to expect that the silliness and lying of these freak journals will be remembered against them? That in the next period of excitement, news-

[8] *Ibid.,* March 21, 1898, 6.
[9] *Ibid.,* 7.
[10] *Ibid.,* March 17, 1898, 1.
[11] *Idem.*
[12] *Idem.*
[13] *The Nation,* LXVI, May 5, 1898, 334.
[14] *Idem.*
[15] *Idem.*
[16] Indianapolis *Journal,* Feb. 26, 1898, 4; *Chronicle,* Feb. 18, 1898, 6.
[17] *Sentinel,* April 18, 1898, 4.

paper readers will remember that if you read it in a yellow journal, it probably isn't so.

The public should realize that there are two kinds of newspapers—those which try to get the news, and those which habitually reject the news on the ground that it is not sufficiently sensational, and then fill their columns with conjectures and guesses.

Quite as denunciatory of sensational newspapers as Godkin was Walter Wellman, correspondent for the Chicago *Times-Herald.* Referring to the practices of "certain newspapers in both the East and West," Wellman wrote:[18]

Every hour rumors of one sort or another float through the air of Washington. Some newspapers investigate these wild yarns, and if any published account of them is given it is only in an inconspicuous way and accompanied by authoritative denials. Other newspapers, some of which are printed in Chicago and get most of their so-called news from New York, treat these unconfirmed rumors as the most important and significant news of the day. Many public officials here condemn the sensational newspapers for harrowing public opinion far beyond the needs of the case. One striking instance of the harm which these sensational and irresponsible journals can do is found in New York. Administrative officials have been hoping the Spanish cruiser Vizcaya would stop out of New York harbor. Assistant Secretary of the Navy Roosevelt yesterday wrote a letter to the chief of police of New York, asking the co-operation of that official in averting a possible attack upon the Vizcaya. In this letter Secretary Roosevelt pointed out that one New York newspaper had virtually invited misguided men to destroy the Vizcaya.

Wellman, in discussing newspaper "fakes," asserted that Key West almost since the beginning of hostilities in Cuba had been "not the seat of war, but of war correspondents:"[19]

Much of the excitement that the people of the United States have manifested over the Cuban affairs has

---

[18] *Times-Herald,* Feb. 19, 1898, 2.
[19] *Ibid.,* 6.

resulted from special dispatches sent out from Key West by correspondents of sensational newspapers.

Many people accept the statements contained in these special dispatches without questioning the correspondents' motives or facilities for attaining facts. An illustration of this was had the other day when a dispatch from there gave what purported to be a description done to the hull of the battleship Maine before divers sent down by Captain Sigsbee could have completed an examination. Readers unfamiliar with the methods of collecting and distributing news believed that the dispatch was founded upon actual discoveries made through official investigation of the cause of the disaster.

Almost since the beginning of hostilities between Spain and Cuba, Key West has been the seat, not of war, but of war correspondents. From that vantage ground of safety writers who never set foot on Cuban soil sent out thrilling descriptions of battles which they claimed to have witnessed. Government secrets and the plans of both armies were revealed in a manner calculated to convince the reader that the correspondent had the full confidence of all the civil and military officials on the island.

Subsequent events disproved nearly every sensational story sent out from Key West, but there seems to have been no abatement in the pernicious activity of the writers who rely upon their imaginations for "news."

To what extent the Key West correspondents have been influenced by their sympathies and the Cuban Junta is a matter of varying opinion. While the officials' headquarters of the Junta are in New York, the base of official operation is Key West.

The New Orleans *Times-Democrat,* in asserting that many of the news reports concerning the Maine disaster were unreliable, said that on all such occasions "fervid imaginations come into play where facts are unobtainable; and often it is difficult to know where fancy ends and fact begins."[20] Referring to the publication of the "suppressed" cable dis-

[20] *Times-Democrat,* Feb. 18, 1898, 4.

patch, which sensational newspapers said had been sent by Captain Sigsbee to Secretary Long concerning the cause of the explosion of the Maine, the *Times-Democrat* remarked:[21]

> No doubt the wonderful dispatch was "suppressed" to all the journalistic world but the *World* and the *Journal;* nothing is "suppressed" to them—they can smell a secret dispatch, if they do not see it.

The *Times-Democrat* charged that an Associated Press correspondent had contributed his quota of fiction to the discoveries reported after the Maine disaster. Quoting an Associated Press dispatch which stated that divers working about the bottom of the Maine had discovered an eight-inch percussion hole in her plate, the New Orleans paper said:[22]

> This information is even more interesting than that evolved from the inner consciousness of the journals. We have had no news as yet that "divers have been working about her bottom," so as to discover eight-inch percussion holes in her bow plates. The work of the divers will, of course, not commence until the committee of inquiry, which has been already appointed, has begun its investigation; the divers will then play a most important role and will probably furnish the information on which the committee of inquiry will mainly rely in arriving at their decision. But until that committee shall have taken hold, irresponsible divers will not be allowed to monkey around the half-submerged ship; they might render difficult if not impossible the means of arriving at a decision.

Criticizing the "irresponsible and reckless" manner in which "certain New York papers" had conducted their policies with regard to the Maine explosion, the Boston *Herald,* which was not above reproach in this respect as the files for this period show, stated that these papers had become "notorious for furnishing fake news."[23] The trouble with the Cuban dispatches, the *Herald* said, was that "both sides seem to indulge in the tallest kind of lying."[24]

[21] *Idem.*
[22] *Idem.*
[23] Boston *Herald,* March 4, 1898, 6.
[24] *Ibid.,* July 28, 1896, 12.

The Washington *Post* also discussed "yellow journalism," referring to the secrecy of the investigation of the Maine disaster as furnishing a great opportunity to sensational newspapers to exploit fakes and mislead the public.[25] Pending the inquiry into the cause of the explosion, "yellow" journals, the *Post* said, contrived exaggerated news stories, and enterprising news agencies and correspondents sent out from Havana "materials from any view of the matter the reader may prefer."[26]

Obviously, many of the newspapers unsuspectingly carried unreliable news dispatches. Some of the papers, while publishing these false reports, denounced in editorials such exaggerated news articles. It is improbable, however, that occasional editorial denouncements of sensational practices were sufficient to neutralize the effect of the daily display of dispatches concerning Spanish atrocities.

Both Pulitzer and Hearst strongly favored the cause of the Cubans—the former because the issue of liberty was involved; he was engaged in bitter rivalry with Hearst; and besides he "rather liked the idea of war, not a big one, but one that would arouse interest and give him a chance to gauge the reflex in his circulation figures."[27] Hearst was equally interested in his circulation figures and welcomed the "sporadic outbursts of groups of patriots in Cuba who were agitating for freedom from Spanish rule."[28]

The conflict with Spain has often been referred to as "Hearst's War," but this accusation is manifestly unjust in view of the activities of such newspapers as Pulitzer's *World,* Dana's *Sun,* Bennett's *Herald,* Medill's *Tribune,* and many less powerful publications in all parts of the nation. Pulitzer originally set the pace in exploiting the Cuban rebellion, only to be oustripped by Hearst and beaten at his own practice. As Oswald Garrison Villard so aptly expressed it:[29]

> It was by this appeal to the basest passions of the crowd that Mr. Pulitzer succeeded; like many another

---

[25] Washington *Post,* Feb. 25, 1898, 4.
[26] *Idem.*
[27] Don C. Seitz, *Joseph Pulitzer His Life and Letters* (New York, 1924), 238.
[28] John K. Winkler, *W. R. Hearst—An American Phenomenon* (New York, 1928), 148.
[29] Oswald Garrison Villard, *Some Newspapers and Newspapermen* (New York, 1923), 44-45.

he deliberately stooped for success, and then, having achieved it, slowly put on garments of righteousness.

The sensational press had finally triumphed. Led by the *World* and *Journal*, partisan newspapers, after carefully arranging the stage for the final act in the drama of war propaganda, "played up" the Maine explosion without restraint and left the American public reeling from a bombardment of half-truths, misstatement of facts, rumors, and faked dispatches. Sensing the popular tide, a hesitant administration, egged on by a "jingo" Congress, proposed war with a nation already on the verge of collapse from internal strife and rebellion.

SELECT BIBLIOGRAPHY

I. DOCUMENTS

Congressional Record, XXVIII, XXIX, XXX, XXXI, December, 1896-April, 1898.

Cuban Affairs, 1897. 54 Congress, 2 Session, *Senate Document* No. 40.

Foreign Relations of the United States, 1896-1898.

Hinds, Ascher C. *Precedents of the House of Representatives*, IV.

House Journal. 54 Congress, 1 Session, 1895-1896; 54 Congress, 2 Session, 1896-1897; 55 Congress, 2 Session, 1897-1898.

Message of the President of the United States, Communicated to the Two Houses of Congress, on the Relations of the United States to Spain by Reason of the Warfare in the Island of Cuba. 55 Congress, 2 Session, *House Document* No. 405.

Report of the Census of Cuba, 1900.

Richardson, James D. *A Compilation of the Messages and Papers of Presidents*, 1789-1897, IX.

Senate Journal. 54 Congress, 1 Session, 1895-1896; 54 Congress, 2 Session, 1896-1897; 55 Congress, 2 Session, 1897-1898.

Spanish Diplomatic Correspondence and Documents, 1896-1900 (Translation). Washington, 1905.

Speeches and Documents on Cuba. 54 Congress, 1 Session, *Senate Report* No. 141.

II. GENERAL WORKS

Alfonso, Manuel F. and Martinez, T. Valero. *Cuba Before the World.* New York, 1915.

Alger, Russell A. *The Spanish-American War.* New York, 1901.

Allport, Floyd Henry. *Social Psychology.* New York, 1924.

The Group Fallacy. Hanover, N. H., 1927.

Angell, Norman. *The Public Mind.* New York, 1927.

Associated Press, *By-Laws Relating to Stockholders and Members of*, 1895; 1897. N.p., n.d.

Second Annual Report, 1902, of the Board of Directors to the Members. New York, 1902.

Atkins, Edwin F. *Sixty Years in Cuba.* Cambridge, 1926.

Ayer, N. W. & Son's. *American Newspaper Annual, 1895-1898.* Philadelphia, 1898.

Bassett, John Spencer. *Expansion and Reform, 1889-1926.* New York, 1929.

Beer, Thomas, *The Mauve Decade; American Life at the End of the Nineteenth Century.* New York, 1926.

Hanna. New York, 1929.

Bent, Silas. *Ballyhoo; The Voice of the Press.* New York, 1928.

Benton, Elbert J. *International Law and Diplomacy of the Spanish-American War.* Baltimore, 1908.

Bernays, Edward L. *Crystallizing Public Opinion.* New York, 1923.

Propaganda. New York, 1928.

Bishop, Joseph Bucklin. *Theodore Roosevelt and His Time Shown in His Own Letters.* New York, 1920.

Bleyer, Willard Grosvenor. *Main Currents in the History of American Journalism.* New York, 1927.

Bryce, James. *The American Commonwealth.* Vol. II. New York, 1908.

Burton, Theodore E. *John Sherman.* New York, 1906.

Callahan, James Morton. *Cuba and International Relations; A Historical Study in American Diplomacy.* Baltimore, 1899.

Chadwick, French Ensor. *The Relations of the United States and Spain.* New York, 1909.

Channing, Edward. *A History of the United States.* New York, 1905.

Chapman, Charles Edward. *A History of the Cuban Republic; A Study in Hispanic American Politics.* New York, 1927.

Columbia University Studies in History, Economics and Public Law, No. 227, C, 1921; No. 228, C, 1921; No. 267, CXXI, 1926.

Constitution Establishing Self-government in the Island of Cuba and Porto Rico, Promulgated by Royal Decree of Nov. 25, 1897. (Translated from Spanish). Washington, 1899.

Cortissoz, Royal. *The Life of Whitelaw Reid.* New York, 1921.

Conway, Sir Martin. *The Crowd in Peace and War.* New York, 1915.

Creel, George. *How We Advertised America.* New York, 1920.

Creelman, James. *On the Great Highway; The Wanderings and Adventures of a Special Correspondent.* Boston, 1907.

Croly, Herbert D. *Marcus Alonzo Hanna; His Life and Works.* New York, 1912.

Davis, Elmer. *History of the New York Times 1851-1921.* New York, 1921.

Davis, Richard Harding. *Notes of a War Correspondent.* New York, 1912.

Dennis, Alfred Louis Pinneo. *Adventures in American Diplomacy.* New York, 1928.

Dewey, Davis Rich. *National Problems, 1885-1897.* New York, 1907.

Dewey, John. *The Public and Its Problems.* New York, 1927.

How We Think. Boston, 1910.

Human Nature and Conduct. New York, 1922.

Dickinson, Edwin DeWitt. *The Law of Nations: Cases and Readings.* New York, 1929.

Dorsey, George. *Why We Behave Like Human Beings.* New York, 1925.

Flint, Grover. *Marching With Gomez: A War Correspondent's Field Note-Book, Kept During Four Months With the Cuban Army.* New York, 1898.

Graves, W. Brooke. *Readings in Public Opinion.* New York, 1928.

Ginsberg, Morris. *The Psychology of Society.* New York, 1921.

Hamlin, C. H. *The War Myth in United States History.* New York, 1927.

Hibben, Parton. *The Peerless Leader, William Jennings Bryan.* New York, 1929.

Hobson, John Atkinson. *The Psychology of Jingoism.* London, 1901.

Kent, Frank R. *The Great Game of Politics.* New York, 1923.

Political Behavior. New York, 1928.

Lasswell, Harold D. *Propaganda Technique in the World War.* New York, 1927.

Latanè, John Halladay. *The Diplomacy of the United States in Regard to Cuba.* Washington, 1898.

A History of American Foreign Policy. New York, 1927.

Life and Letters of Edwin Lawrence Godkin. Ed. by Rollo Ogden. New York, 1907.

Lippmann, Walter. *Public Opinion.* New York, 1922.

The Phantom Public. New York, 1925.

Lipsky, Abram. *Man the Puppet; the Art of Controlling Minds.* New York, 1925.

Lodge, Henry Cabot. *The War With Spain.* New York, 1899.

Theodore Roosevelt: Selections from the Correspondence of Theodore Roosevelt and Henry Cabot Lodge, 1884-1918. New York, 1925.

Lowell, A. Lawrence. *Public Opinion in War and Peace.* Cambridge, 1926.

Public Opinion and Popular Government. New York, 1913.

Martin, Everett Dean. *The Behavior of Crowds.* New York, 1920.

Mayo, Lawrence Shaw. *America of Yesterday as Reflected in the Journal of John Davis Long.* Boston, 1923.

McCall, Samuel Walker. *The Life of Thomas Brackett Reed.* Boston, 1914.

Mcdonald, Helen Grace. *Canadian Public Opinion on the American Civil War.* New York, 1926.

McDougall, William. *Introduction to Social Psychology.* Boston, 1926.

The Group Mind. New York, 1920.

McElroy, John. *The Life of Maj. William McKinley.* Washington, 1896.

McElroy, Robert McNutt. *Grover Cleveland, the Man and the Statesman, an Authorized Biography.* New York, 1923.

"*M.E.S.*" *His Book, A Tribute and a Souvenir of the Twenty-five Years, 1893-1918, of the Service of Melville E. Stone as General Manager of the Associated Press.* New York, 1928.

Millis, Walter. *The Martial Spirit.* Cambridge, 1931.

Moore, John Bassett. *A Digest of International Law.* Washington, 1906.

Morgan, John T. *Belligerent Rights for Cuba: Speeches in the Senate of the United States, Jan. 29, 1896-May 4, 1897.* Washington, 1897.

Nevins, Allan. *The Evening Post—A Century of Journalism.* New York, 1922.

Henry White; Thirty Years of American Diplomacy. New York, 1930.

American Press Opinion, Washington to Coolidge; a Documentary Record of Editorial Leadership and Criticism, 1785-1927. New York, 1928.

O'Brien, Frank M. *The Story of the Sun.* New York, 1928.

Odegard, Peter H. *The American Public Mind.* New York, 1930.

Olcott, Charles Sumner. *The Life of William McKinley.* New York, 1916.

Overstreet, H. A. *Influencing Human Behavior.* Norton, 1925.

Parker, George Frederick. *Recollections of Grover Cleveland.* New York, 1909.

Paxson, Frederic L. *Recent History of the United States.* New York, 1921.

Peck, Harry Thurston. *Twenty Years of the Republic.* New York, 1913.

Pierce, Bessie. *Public Opinion and the Teaching of History.* New York, 1926.

Ponsonby, Arthur. *Falsehood in War-Time.* New York, 1928.
Democracy and Diplomacy. London, 1915.

Quesada, Gonzalo de, and Northrop, Henry D. *The War in Cuba: Being a Full Account of Her Great Struggle for Freedom, Containing a Complete Record of Spanish Tyranny and Oppression Together With a Full Description of Cuba.* N.p., 1896.

Randall, J. H., Jr. *Our Changing Civilization.* New York, 1929.

Rhodes, James Ford. *The McKinley and Roosevelt Administrations, 1897-1909.* New York 1922.

Robinson, Albert Gardner. *Cuba, Old and New.* New York, 1915.

Robinson, J. H. *The Mind in the Making.* New York, 1921.

Roosevelt, Theodore. *An Autobiography.* New York, 1913.

Rosewater, Victor. *History of Cooperative News-gathering in the United States.* New York, 1930.

Russell, Bertrand A. W. "Government by Propaganda" in *These Eventful Years.* London, 1924.

Salmon, Lucy Maynard. *The Newspaper and the Historian.* New York, 1923.
The Newspaper and Authority. Oxford, 1923.

Sears, Louis M. *History of American Foreign Relations.* New York, 1928.

Seitz, Don C. *The James Gordon Bennetts Father and Son, Proprietors of the New York Herald.* Indianapolis, 1928.
Joseph Pulitzer, His Life and Letters. New York, 1924.

Thayer, William Roscoe. *The Life and Letters of John Hay.* New York, 1915.

The W-G-N. Published by the Chicago Tribune in Commemoration of Its Seventy-fifth Birthday, 1922.

The Statesman's Yearbook, 1900. London, 1900.

Trotter, W. *Instincts of the Herd in Peace and War.* New York, 1926.

Verrill, Alpheus Hyatt. *Cuba Past and Present.* New York, 1914.

Villard, Oswald Garrison. *Some Newspapers and Newspaper Men.* New York, 1926.

Wallas, Graham. *Human Nature in Politics.* New York, 1921.

Watterson, Henry. *History of the Spanish-American War.* New York, 1898.
"Marse Henry;" An Autobiography. New York, 1919.

White, Elizabeth Brett. *American Opinion of France From Lafayette to Poincarè.* New York, 1927.

Wilson, James Harrison. *The Life of Charles A. Dana.* New York, 1907.

Winkler, John K. *W. R. Hearst—An American Phenomenon.* New York, 1928.

Who's Who in America, 1899-1900. Ed. by John W. Leonard. Chicago, 1900.

Young, Kimball. *Source Book for Social Psychology.* New York, 1927.
Bibliography for Propaganda and Censorship. University of Oregon, 1928.

III. PERIODICALS

ARTICLES:

Connery, Thomas B. "The Collection of News" in *Cosmopolitan Magazine,* XXIII (1897), 21-32.

Godkin, E. L. "The Growth and Expression of Public Opinion" in *The Atlantic Monthly,* LXXXI (1898), 1-15.

Hawley, Walter L. "Development of the American Newspaper" in ***Popular Science Monthly***, LXI (1899), 187-204.

Hazeltine, Mayo W. "What Shall Be Done About Cuba?" in ***North American Review***, *CLXII* (1896), 406-413

Hershey, Amos S. "The Recognition of Cuban Belligerency" in ***Annals of the American Academy***, VII (1896), 450-461.

King, Clarence. "Shall Cuba be Free?" in ***The Forum***, XX (1895), 50-65.

Lodge, Henry Cabot. "Our Duty to Cuba" in ***The Forum***, XXI (1896), 278-287.

Moore, John Bassett. "Cuban Belligerency" in ***The Forum***, XXI (1896), 288-300.

Stone, Melville E. "The Associated Press" in ***Century Magazine*** XLVIII (1905), 299-310.

Reno, George. "Operating an Underground Route to Cuba" in ***Cosmopolitan Magazine***, XXVII (1899), 431-440.

MAGAZINES:

Annals of the American Academy, VII (1896).

Atlantic Monthly, LXXXI (1898).

Century Magazine, XLVIII (1905).

Cosmopolitan Magazine, XXVI, XXVII (1898, 1899).

Harper's Weekly, XXIX, (1895).

Leslie's Weekly, LXXX, LXXXI, LXXXII, (1895-1896).

North American Review, CLXI, CLXII, CLXIII, CLXIV, (1895-1898).

The Forum, XX, XXI (1895-1896).

The Nation, LXVI (1898).

NEWSPAPERS:

Atlanta *Constitution*, 1898.

Boston *Herald*, 1895-1898.

Charleston *News and Courier*, 1895-1898.

Chicago *Times-Herald*, 1895-1898.

Chicago *Inter-Ocean*, 1895-1896.

Chicago *Tribune*, 1895-1898.

Cincinnati *Commercial-Gazette*, 1895-1898.

Indianapolis *Journal*, 1895-1898.

Milwaukee *Sentinel*, 1895-1898.

New Orleans *Times-Democrat*, 1895-1898.

New York *World*, 1895-1898.

New York *Journal*, 1896-1898.

New York *Sun*, 1895-1898.

New York *Herald*, 1895-1898.

New York *Times*, 1895-1898.

San Francisco *Chronicle*, 1895-1898.

Washington *Post*, 1896-1898.

INDEX